I have visited Kaduna, Nigeria, the friend Tunde Bolanta pastors a vibrant church. I have also ministered alongside this humble warrior. His message is relevant for the global church—and especially needed in the Western world where we have forgotten that real Christianity requires sacrifice, and authentic faith requires holiness. I commend this book and pray that Tunde Bolanta's passion for a New Testament revival will spread throughout the world.

—J. LEE GRADY
CONTRIBUTING EDITOR, *CHARISMA MAGAZINE*
DIRECTOR, THE MORDECAI PROJECT

This book is: encouraging, convicting, inspiring, insightful, instructive, crisp, and clean with Holy Spirit sparkle! I want to have all my pastors and many of my friends read it. I want to make it a required study for our rising leaders here in the UK.

Thank you for the privilege of reading this message from your heart. I was captured. It grabbed me with revelation and conviction, so I set it aside to read more carefully and prayerfully. It truly ministered to me. Thanks again, Tunde. It is an honor and a blessing to receive your ministry via this writing.

—H.P. HAROLD G. PRESLEY
INTERNATIONAL PENTECOSTAL HOLINESS CHURCH, UK
AND NORTHWEST EUROPE

With *Spiritual Brokenness*, Pastor Tunde Bolanta challenges much contemporary understanding of life and ministry. From a firm biblical basis he shows that the carnal self has to be broken for God's Spirit to flow freely through a person. The implications of this are set out with clarity through reflections on biblical characters. Reading through *Spiritual Brokenness* one encounters the fruits of a mature walk with God from an apostolic leader. This is not a theoretical book. It is a book written from the heart of a great leader in God's kingdom. I wholeheartedly recommend it.

—Dr. Tonny Jacobsen
Chairman, Free-Church Net, Denmark

SPIRITUAL
BROKENNESS

SPIRITUAL
BROKENNESS

TUNDE BOLANTA

CREATION
HOUSE

SPIRITUAL BROKENNESS by Tunde Bolanta
Published by Creation House Books
A Charisma Media Company
600 Rinehart Road
Lake Mary, Florida 32746
www.charismamedia.com

Unless otherwise noted, all Scripture quotations are from the King James Version of the Bible.

Scripture quotations are also from the Amplified Bible. Old Testament copyright © 1965, 1987 by the Zondervan Corporation. The Amplified New Testament copyright © 1954, 1958, 1987 by the Lockman Foundation. Used by permission.

Design Director: Bill Johnson
Cover design by Nathan Morgan

Visit the author's Web site: www.rbcmonline.org

Library of Congress Control Number: 2011928563
International Standard Book Number: 978-1-61638-591-0

First Edition

11 12 13 14 15 — 9 8 7 6 5 4 3 2 1
Printed in Canada

CONTENTS

1

LEARN TO DIE
IN ORDER TO LIVE

ESUS TAUGHT THAT we cannot be fruitful until we learn how to die.[1] The apostle Paul said, "I die daily."[2] Jesus likened the death of the flesh to the wearing away of the outer shell of a grain of wheat until it becomes rotten or dead, after which a new life begins. When a believer comes to faith in Jesus, he receives eternal life, but his flesh is not saved. The flesh and the mind, unbroken and unrenewed, will cause believers to fail and be unfruitful.

The apostle James stressed the importance of having our being under control. He said we put a bridle in a horse's mouth to control its body and give direction.[3] An unbroken horse is dangerous to the rider. A believer may have given his life to Christ, but without spiritual brokenness he could be likened to a horse that is unbroken. Our flesh can be compared to the unbroken horse, wild and undisciplined. We are incapable of manifesting God's glory in this state. Our lives have little impact in this state; our lights are placed under a bushel.

Little wonder the Bible refers to this type of believer as carnal or natural.[4] Looking at this kind of believer you would not be able to differentiate between him and an unsaved person. Outside of religious activities, this believer is no different from the unsaved and cannot be said to be a real light. While it is unfortunate for a believer to live in this state, it is a tragedy for a minister to live this way, because he would be a stumbling block to many. Jesus said men do not light a candle and put it under a bushel.[5] The bushel is the flesh that hinders the glory of God from being seen.

Spiritual brokenness is important for all believers, because when a believer is not fruitful he has no impact on the world as salt and light. A person who has a ministry calling must either walk in brokenness, or else become dangerously contagious. In the ministry, an unbroken vessel is much like an unbroken horse who is self-willed, or controlled by the flesh. A horse has great power, but unbroken it becomes a danger to all. The minister has a holy calling, and the Holy Spirit is in and upon him. This is the same responsibility God gave to Jesus, and He manifested the glory of God. Brokenness in the life of Jesus was the key reason God was able to release so much glory through Him.

Jesus came to the Jordan River to be baptized by John the

Baptist, who was His forerunner. In other words, He submitted Himself to John. This action stunned John because he knew Jesus was greater than he, and his entire ministry was to announce the arrival of and prepare the way for Jesus. Jesus had no problems with submission to others in the ministry, because He was secure in His identity in God.

Jesus's decision to come to the earth and leave His glory is a manifestation of spiritual brokenness; it is dying to any personal agenda, name, or fame. He laid aside His majesty to become a man, to take on the nature of sin and suffer all the consequences. Jesus made Himself of no reputation[6] in order to fulfill the will of God. Being baptized by John was nothing compared to this. This mind-set is a requirement for effectiveness in life and ministry. To walk in the glory of God, however, requires dying daily, putting the flesh under, and developing a lifestyle of righteousness. Brokenness is a key to kingdom advancement. This is diametrically opposed to the system of the world that believers walked in before.

When people are insecure about their identity in God, submission becomes an issue in life and ministry. This is the outer shell, the flesh that needs to experience death. Who we are in Christ precedes who we are in ministry; apart from Christ you have no ministry. Submission to the order the Father has established causes pride to be broken. Ministers can make the mistake of putting their office before relationship with God. It is important to note that the affirmation of the Father followed the demonstration of brokenness before Jesus could be released into the ministry.

After the baptism of Jesus in the Jordan, a voice was heard

from heaven. It was the Father saying, "This is my beloved son, with whom I am well pleased."[7] The Father spoke of Him as a son, not as the Messiah. The Holy Spirit also came upon Him, and so began His ministry. He was the Son of God from age one to age thirty, but brokenness qualified Him as a son before God placed the anointing on Him. This should be a model for all ministers: that we desire brokenness, which is a hallmark of sonship, before ministry. Jesus learned obedience through the things He suffered.[8]

Taking on human nature, being rejected by His people, being misunderstood by His family, waiting on His ministry, ministering only as a man anointed by the Holy Spirit, and enduring reproach from the religious leaders of His day are some of the things Christ suffered daily. But He chose to yield to the Father always, to put His flesh under daily, and to walk in godliness as a lifestyle.

Brokenness is a progressive journey, and we need to be open for God to work in each of the many areas of our lives. It is instructive that baby Jesus was seen by the shepherds in the manger, while the wise men saw a child in the house, and the rabbis saw Him at age twelve in the temple, while He was not yet ready to minister. The declaration and subsequent empowerment by God of the Lord Jesus is the culmination of a journey of obedience through the things He suffered. Brokenness is a journey to becoming Christlike, in which the flesh is put to death daily. Jesus knew His commission and destination, but He submitted to His parents. After astounding all the religious leaders in the temple, Jesus went home and submitted. He waited for the fullness of time and submitted to John the Baptist, and God released Him.

In today's world, Jesus would have been taunted about His paternity. Those who remembered that their children were slaughtered on account of His birth would have resented Him. Many of His age group were dead at birth. He probably did not have many mates His age to play with. Nonetheless, He did not allow His flesh to get in the way. He waited for God.

Submitting to other people's ministry can be a challenge for those who measure themselves against others. They are happy as long as there is no one they feel is doing better, or who is bigger than them. They have a morbid desire and compulsion to look better and do better than others. Their competitiveness is born out of a feeling of inadequacy. Jesus knew He was sent by God. He had only one desire—to obey God—and it was of no consequence to Him how other people interpreted His obedience. Believers and ministers who are insecure in their identity need the approval of men, but Jesus only needed the approval of the Father. The Father was pleased.

Immediately after His baptism, Jesus was led into the wilderness to be tempted by the devil. This means Satan challenged Him to see if He would yield to the flesh. Before He was released into a ministry that has changed humanity, He was tempted in many areas, yet He did not fail. The apostle James taught believers to submit to God and resist the devil.[9] At the Jordan River during His baptism, Jesus submitted to God. He walked in submission and brokenness and was prepared to take on the devil in the wilderness.

Jesus was very secure in His identity and relationship with

5

the Father, so much so that He did not struggle to be known, and did not advertise His miracles. He healed many, and instructed them to tell no man. He was not seeking political relevance. His followers would have been happy had He led a revolt against the oppressive Romans, but He had no interest in this. Ministers today do not only use the ministry as a platform for self-promotion, but exaggeration has become the order of the day. Some are even prepared to *fake* it if they can't *faith* it. God is not moving and doing miracles to make us look good, but He is confirming His Word and meeting people's needs because He loves them. When Jesus mixed with the high and mighty, He was focused on their salvation and the kingdom of God; He was not there for personal advantage. Ministers should be careful not to sacrifice their integrity for political relevance and personal advantage. Your security is not based on how many high-profile people are in your church, or how many of these people recognize you.

It is not uncommon for believers and ministers to participate in name-dropping in an attempt to convince others that they have successful people around them, and are well connected. It is important to know that God is not moved by the big names. He is only concerned about you doing His will. If the so-called successful person does not fear God, and you dote on him or her for material advantage, you dishonor the anointing of God and the ministry in so doing. Many people on whom the Lord has placed the anointing have lost it due to their attachment to money and material advantage. This shows a lack of brokenness. The flesh is still running the lives of such people. It is more important that heaven knows you than to have your name mentioned in the corridors of power. The flesh is crucified with her lusts and desire on the cross. Desire or lust for human recognition, lust for power, and pride of life are works of the flesh that hinder the glory of God in our lives. Jesus was not evaluating Himself by human parameters; otherwise He would not have submitted to the baptism of John. Jesus was concerned about fulfilling the will of God. This example of submission and humility is a far cry from what we see today, when ministers want to have the same status as Hollywood stars.

Paul did not focus on his material goods. He never mentioned or listed his human achievements to boast, but said he counted them as dung. Why is it that the yardstick we use to measure success in life and ministry today measures material accomplishments, rather than the impact made on lives and the sacrifices made by God's servants? The early church noted and recognized Barnabas and Paul as men who hazarded their lives for the gospel.[10] Their material status was inconsequential.

May I state clearly that the gospel cannot move forward without finances, but using money, or the lack of it, to judge the will of God is unscriptural. Money is a low form of power. If God cannot trust a person to live a life free of immorality, and the person parades wealth as an indication of divine acceptance, this person is a carnal believer who should not be filling a pulpit in the first place. In addition, to walk in dominion over your flesh in every area except your finances would limit your ministry.

Religion says money is evil, but it is actually the love of money that the Scriptures instruct us to avoid.[11] You don't need to have a lot of money to love it. Those who love money live for it. The size of their bank account determines their joy. How much of it they have is a reflection of their status in life. Their value of human life is tied to money. They find it difficult to give, and when they do give, they help those who can give them something back. Their money becomes an idol. Money is much like manure: When you spread it out, it brings growth. Heap it on yourself, and you stink.

Brokenness allows us to keep things in perspective. One of the best illustrations of brokenness is the donkey Jesus rode into Jerusalem.[12] This donkey was tied up at an intersection. The owners had never used it, but now the Master had need of it. Jesus rode on it immediately. Ordinarily this would have resulted in an accident, because it was not broken; it was untrained. The posture of a donkey teaches us some things about brokenness. The donkey is lowly in disposition. It bears the burden of transporting others and luggage day in, day out. Jesus asked us to learn from Him because He was meek and lowly.

No man can get on a horse and ride at once. It takes time to break the horse. This donkey Jesus asked His disciples to bring was tied down because it had not yet been broken. The owners had not put it to use. Many wonder why the Lord will not use them, but they may have not submitted themselves to the daily discipline of brokenness. God is not looking for perfect vessels. As soon as we sign up, He begins to work in us to release His glory. When we are corrected by the Word, when tested or troubled, we must yield to the Lord to produce godly character. Have you ever tried to defend yourself after someone said something untrue about you? Maybe you thought you did a good job only to hear something worse. Eventually you turned everything over to God, and everything was OK. In this situation, you had to learn to forgive and not worry. You learned that you were a donkey whose defense comes from the Master.

When God begins to use you as a believer, you are grateful because you are walking in higher purpose, but your willingness is what made this possible. In order for the Lord to continually use the believer, he must daily live to do the will of God; he must submit to the Lord, who is the Rider. When we love Him, it becomes a joy to live this way. God is not a taskmaster. The flesh may see this as a death, but it is required for fruit to come out of our lives.

As Jesus rode into Jerusalem to fulfill His purpose, the donkey had the experience of people casting down their garments before him. It was a glorious occasion. As He served the Lord He walked in the glory, but He remembered He was only a servant. True, we are sons of God, but the Bible admonishes us to have the mind of a servant like Jesus, who was humble and impacted the world.[13] God gave this admonition because He knows that our minds and bodies are not saved and unbroken. They become our worst enemy and limit our effectiveness. After a horse's owner has the animal for a long time, he develops a telepathic connection with the horse. A simple movement of the owner, and the horse responds. We must become so intimate with the Father as sons of God that His thoughts are the same as our thoughts. This happens as we read the Word and worship daily. As we yield to the leadings of God in our own spirit, His thoughts and ours become one.

- A broken horse is a servant at heart, bearing the burden of others and transporting people and luggage.

- The donkey must have a lowly disposition, a form of meekness, in order to do her assignment.

- Every saved person has an unbroken part of his mind and flesh that must be tamed before he can be fruitful.

- A broken horse is grateful that the Lord found him and unchained him and released him into destiny.

- A broken horse is not self-willed.

- A broken horse cannot be in competition with the rider.

- Brokenness and willingness to follow the Lord will cause others to celebrate the Lord in our lives, just as the donkey carried Jesus and people worshiped the Lord.

- A broken horse is promoted and walks where the Lord walks, but remembers he is a donkey.

- A broken horse does not share the accolades of his master.
- A broken horse knows the limelight is over when the work is done.
- A broken horse is intimate with the rider.
- A broken horse knows the value of rest before the next assignment.
- A broken horse knows she will ride wherever the Master goes, as long as she is available.
- A broken horse must keep in step with the rider—not too fast and not too slow.
- The broken horse is not seeking limelight, but service.

A Crucified Life

Kathryn Kuhlman gives the testimony of how she experienced brokenness and became more effective for the kingdom.

In that moment, with the tears streaming down my face, then looking up and vowing, He and I made each other promises. There are some things that you don't talk about. There are some things that are so sacred, you just don't talk about those things. There are just some things that are terrifically personal between the two of you. It's like some things that are just so personal between a husband and wife, you just don't display them out in public. He knows that I'll be true to Him as long as my old heart will keep beating. And I know that I'll be true to Him. We have a pact, and it's all settled. At the end of a dead-end street, four o'clock on Saturday afternoon—in that moment when I yielded to Him body, soul, and spirit, when I gave Him everything, all there was of me, I knew then, beloved, what the scripture meant, and you'll never change the meaning of it: "If any man will follow Me, let him take up his cross." (See Matthew 16:24.) Beloved, the cross is always the sign, the symbol, of death. It's the symbol of death! That afternoon, "Kathryn Kuhlman" died. I mean died! Kathryn Kuhlman died! If I were to tell you that I don't even associate that name with myself...I tell you the truth, I died. If you've never had that death to the flesh, you don't know what I'm talking [about]...There're some of you who know. [14]

The new creation in Christ has been crucified and raised up with Christ. An understanding of what really took place on the cross is key to living in victory. The cross was the place of death, an exchange.

Let us consider this illustration. A man has been given up to die, and he needs a heart transplant. Another man decides to give his own heart to the sick man, but to give away his heart means he has to die. He agrees to die, but with certain conditions: that the sick man would willingly live out his own dreams, and live the way he would have lived. When the sick man receives the new heart, he has also died in the sense that, though he is alive, he is living with a borrowed heart. It is not his; he is living for one other than himself. He only lives to please the one who gave him the new heart. This illustration is similar to what happens to every believer. Jesus gave us His own life. We died with Him on the cross, and the new life that we have now can only be lived for Him in order to be fruitful. We must go back to the cross, the place of death and exchange, before we can truly live for Him. But our flesh, untrained and unsaved, wants to continue to live for itself. Brokenness is the manifestation of a crucified life. Knowing that our old man has been crucified and our new life is not our own, we are not debtors to the flesh. The flesh must die daily, and we must visit the cross and acknowledge that when we received life from Jesus, we died in order to live a resurrected life only for Him.

This is what it means to take up the cross daily, to walk in the spirit. This is what Miss Kuhlman experienced, and each believer needs to accept daily that at the cross the old man ceased to live. The new man only lives to fulfill the wishes of Jesus. Attempting to live a resurrected life without accepting that you died on the cross is putting the cart before the horse. Consider the following scriptures:

> I am crucified with Christ: nevertheless I live; yet not I, but Christ liveth in me: and the life which I now live in the flesh I live by the faith of the Son of God, who loved me, and gave himself for me.
> —GALATIANS 2:20

> For ye are dead and your life is hid with Christ in God.
> —COLOSSIANS 3:3

Knowing this, that our old man is crucified with him, that the body of sin might be destroyed, that henceforth we should not serve sin.

—Romans 6:6

Likewise reckon ye also yourselves to be dead indeed unto sin, but alive unto God through Jesus Christ our Lord.

—Romans 6:11

Therefore, brethren, we are debtors, not to the flesh, to live after the flesh.

—Romans 8:12

2

BROKENNESS: GOD'S PROCESS FOR CHAMPIONS

JACOB, PETER, AND PAUL

SPIRITUAL BROKENNESS IS a progressive work, but there are encounters that are milestones in our lives where definite changes are wrought in the life of the believer. The ultimate goal in the life of every believer should be to become like Christ. The Lord Jesus Himself told us that we cannot be fruitful until we become like the grain of seed that falls to the ground and dies. In the death of the seed, brokenness is experienced, and new life is released. Every life that can impact the lives of others must experience this process.

It is progressive, but there are encounters that mark turning points in our dealings with God. They produce brokenness, which allows us to move farther in our journey toward becoming Christlike. In some cases God removes the mask, and we are confronted with ourselves. In these situations all the bridges are burned, and there are no escape routes. The believer either changes or faces dire consequences. It is like being between the proverbial devil and the deep sea.

JACOB

Jacob was determined from the womb to be a fighter. He grabbed his brother's heel, which is the meaning of his name, "supplanter." By grabbing a person's heel, you cause them to fall, or overcome them. He had an inborn ability to outwit and out-muscle others. He lived out the true meaning of his name. He outwitted his brother when he convinced Esau to sell his birthright for a bowl of pottage, and with the connivance of his mother he received the blessing of the firstborn. He had a great destiny in God, but not until God brought him through the school of brokenness would he be ready to fulfill his destiny.

A cheat and a deceiver *par excellence*, the outcome of his smart deal meant he had to leave home unprepared, to escape the anger of his brother. As providence would have it, he ended up in the house of Laban, an uncle who shared the family trait of cunning. His uncle put him to work, changing his wages ten times. He deceived him and on his wedding night gave him his older daughter, Leah, in place of Rachel, Jacob's preferred choice. To marry his true love, Jacob spent another seven years working under Laban.

Twenty years later, when Jacob decided to return home, his past mistakes and deceptions were waiting for him, as he had to face Esau, his older brother whom he had cheated. Jacob had plotted his escape plan, relying on his natural skills and wit. He arranged for presents to be sent ahead of him, and his family followed. As he waited alone the night before he was to meet face to face with Esau, an angel wrestled with Jacob until the breaking of day, dislocating Jacob's hip in the process. He had his encounter with God.[1]

Hosea 12:3–4[2] relays how Jacob must have prayed; he wept; he made supplication. He had come to the end of the road. His wit could not deliver him. He had run from Laban and now had to confront the ghost of his past. Why did the angel wrestle him? It was simply to break him. The goal was to bring Jacob to the end of Jacob. God wanted to bring him to the end of human strength and confront him with the reality of his real nature. Jacob must have done a lot of heart searching. He must have ruminated on all the events that transpired between him and Esau. He must have remembered Laban's deception and mistreatment. His own character had been tested in that he stayed with Laban and did not elope with Rachel. He felt he had made some improvement in character, but why was the ghost of his past still haunting him? The angel wrestled with him in order to confront him with the truth. God needed to weaken him in order to strengthen him.

The angel asked Jacob a question that rattled him: "What is your name?" For the Israelites, one's name was a reflection of his destiny and identity. The Amplified Bible says that

Jacob answered "in shock of realization" that his name was Jacob, which means "supplanter." God made sure Jacob realized he had been living as a cheat, using his wit and strength to make things happen. The realization of his name, his life, and his inabilities occasioned by the dislocation of his hip drove home the point.

Jacob left with a dislocated hip and a life-changing revelation. He found an opponent that he could not outwit or out-muscle. Jacob asked and wrestled for the right reason this time. He wanted God's blessings, as the things he had obtained by struggle only brought him sorrow. With the impending confrontation with his brother, Jacob had come to the end of Jacob.

Many times when believers are confronted with challenges they want to get out of the problem fast, and wrestle their way through without dealing with the character question involved. Had Jacob wrestled with the angel without the revelation of his character and name—which needed to change—the goal would have been defeated. There are traits of the flesh that are recurring in the lives of believers that must be removed in order for believers to fulfill their destinies. When we face challenges that call our character into question, God is more interested in our character than our comfort. Jacob knew how to wrestle his way out of situations from the womb. He grabbed Esau's heel, and he seemed to be gaining an upper hand in the wrestling match between himself and the angel. His thigh was dislocated, but he held on to the angel. Jacob requested the blessing of the Lord, knowing that he had been fighting a divine being, and that the challenge ahead was beyond him.

God blessed him by causing him to shift his dependency off of himself and onto God. His supplication was heard that night, as he shed tears in prayer, surrendered, and was broken. As he limped away from the presence of God, he had been blessed—but now he walked with a limp, leaning heavily on God, not on his wit or strength. What an irony to win the victory with a limp; but God weakened him in order to teach him to rest in God's ability. With a limp he could not make a quick retreat, but he was able to limp forward into his destiny. He found mercy, because, contrary to his expectation, Esau received him without a fight.

Many a believer may feel disadvantaged because of certain unfortunate events of the past. For this reason the believer feels he needs to pray more, talk less, study the Word more, and progress with fear and trembling. That disadvantage, or limp, produces a dependence on God that is a pole vault into the maturation of his true destiny in God.[3]

PETER

Brokenness is a process God takes His children through to prepare them for their assignments. The apostle Peter was no exception to this process. Peter originally had a common Jewish name, Simon or Simeon, meaning "hearing." He was a native of Bethsaida, the son of Jonas, a fisherman, a trade Peter and his younger brother Andrew embraced. Peter was brought to Jesus by Andrew, and the Lord gave him the name Peter (John 1:42), a reference to the boldness and firmness of his character and his activity in promoting his Master's cause. He received a second call and began to accompany Jesus at the Sea of Galilee near his residence. Thenceforth he learned to be a "fisher of men." (See Matthew 4:18–20; Luke 5:1–11.)

Many remarkable incidents are recorded in the Gospels that illustrate his character. Peter was impulsive, boastful, a natural leader and spokesperson, independent, highly opinionated, and very bold. It was Peter who stepped out onto the water when all the others stayed put in the comfort of the boat. He walked on water toward Jesus, a feat no other disciple performed. Peter answered the question about who Jesus was; he declared that Jesus was the Messiah, a revelation of God's salvation to humanity. Peter was at the Mount of Transfiguration and saw the glory of God. He was present when Jesus raised Jairus's daughter from the dead. When multitudes left Jesus because of His teachings, Peter was the spokesman for the disciples, confirming to Jesus that they were following for the long haul, and were committed to Him in covenant. He did not agree that Jesus should go and end His life on the cross, and told Him so. When the Lord reiterated His resolve to lay down His life and warned the disciples that their faith would fail, Peter declared that even if all others failed, he was ready to die for his Lord. Peter matched his words with action by cutting Malchus's ear off during the arrest of Jesus. Thankfully, Jesus was there to heal the ear.

Peter's breaking point began after the arrest of Jesus, and all disciples fled, as Jesus had foretold.[4] Peter made it to the palace, where he was questioned about his relationship with Jesus by people who recognized him; but his courage failed in the line of fire, and he denied Jesus. He went out and he wept bitterly, as he realized that he was not as strong as he thought, not as bold as he proclaimed, not as faithful as he vowed. In the exact moment when the cock crowed, as Jesus prophesied, Jesus turned to look at Peter. Jesus was facing the greatest trial of His life, the biggest test to His will, but He remembered Peter in his spiritual pilgrimage. This was the moment of Peter's brokenness, an encounter he never forgot. Although Peter had failed to heed the word of the Lord to pray and be watchful, and though he failed to take on board the prophetic warning from the Lord that Satan wanted to sift him, the Lord Jesus still remembered Peter.[5]

The Lord looked at Peter not to condemn him, but as the refiner of silver who has put the silver in the heat of the fire watches it so it is not burned. A refiner of silver was once asked how he would know when the product was ready. He replied to the question, saying it was ready when he could see his reflection in the product. The goal of brokenness is for us to become like Jesus. The Lord continues to watch over us, even in our struggles. The refiner of silver must keep his eye on the product while it is in the midst of the flame. God has also promised we shall not be tested beyond what we can stand. He would never allow the fire to be too hot to destroy us. This is the message of Malachi 3:3.[6]

Jesus knew Peter was sorry, but had faith in him that he would come through. Peter once thought he was bravery personified. He was very sure that he had the moral constitution and backbone to withstand any attack that would come against Jesus, but his confidence was misplaced. His bravado was in the flesh. He needed to learn to lean on the Lord. He needed to put his faith in divine ability, not human ego. For this to happen, the Lord allowed him to fail. Peter denied Christ three times. Peter's failure showed his weakness, but this also led to the realization that he could not survive by human strength. When we place our faith in ourselves, we are most vulnerable. Peter failed where he was most naturally endowed; his boldness and courage could not survive the attack.[7] Skills, gifts, training, and physical attributes must be laid on the altar.

Another example comes to mind. King David was a man who knew the ethics of war, but he was caught napping when his soldiers went to war. He found Bathsheba, and so began his ruin. He had fought so many wars and was familiar with victory; he could predict a war but had no business being at home at that time—worse still cohabiting with the wife of one of his most gallant soldiers. War was his forte and specialty. He killed Goliath, and the women sang that he was more accomplished than King Saul. But the area of his greatest strength was the same area in which he failed.

There are no specialists in life and ministry. True success comes through daily dependence on the grace of God, walking humbly before the Lord in brokenness.[8]

PETER'S REPENTANCE: ANDREW MURRAY'S COMMENTS

"And the Lord turned, and looked upon Peter. And Peter remembered the word of the Lord, how he had said unto him, Before the cock crow, thou shalt deny

me thrice. And Peter went out, and wept bitterly"
(Luke 22:61–62).

That was the turning-point in the history of Peter.
Christ had said to him: "Thou canst not follow me
now." Peter was not in a fit state to follow Christ,
because he had not been brought to an end of himself; he did not know himself, and he therefore could
not follow Christ. But when he went out and wept bitterly, then came the great change. Christ previously
said to him: "When thou art converted, strengthen
thy brethren." Here is the point where Peter was converted from self to Christ. I thank God for the story
of Peter. I do not know a man in the Bible who gives
us greater comfort. When we look at his character,
so full of failures, and at what Christ made him by
the power of the Holy Ghost, there is hope for every
one of us. But remember, before Christ could fill
Peter with the Holy Spirit and make a new man of
him, he had to go out and weep bitterly; he had to
be humbled. If we want to understand this, I think
there are four points that we must look at. First, let
us look at Peter the devoted disciple of Jesus; next, at
Peter as he lived the life of self; then at Peter in his
repentance; and last, at what Christ made of Peter by
the Holy Spirit.[9]

When our natural ability fails us, we are weakened, but
this can be turned around when we look to Him for His
strength. Peter had no doubt that he had blown it. The Lord
looked at him not to condemn him but to bring realization

and truth to dawn on him, much like the angel who asked Jacob what his name was; "in shock of realization" he knew his own character. Peter was confronted with himself. He saw his weaknesses and failures. He saw his real image in the mirror of life, though he thought it was a far cry from how he lived. He was desperate for change. Peter was certainly a work in progress.

Jesus sought Peter after the Resurrection. When the Lord rose from the dead, He sent a special message to Peter through the women who came to the grave. The message to Peter after the Resurrection was to reassure him that he was loved and was not alone.

Jesus gave the disciples breakfast after the Resurrection, but had a conversation with Peter to help him. Three times He asked Peter if he loved Him.[10] In the first two questions, Jesus uses the strong verb *agapan*, while Peter replied with the weaker *philein*. In the third question Jesus uses Peter's word, *philein*. Peter's past failure where he had denied the Lord three times was fresh in his mind. He knew God was calling him to an unconditional love, the love that was ready to lay down his life for the other, just as Jesus did for the world. Peter, after his experience with denying the Lord, did not use the word for unconditional love to answer the Lord. He was honest, because his love—which he thought was unconditional—had failed him. He had betrayed his Friend and Master. This realization is the beginning of the journey of grace. When we realize that nothing good dwells in our flesh, and that our best effort is not good enough without God's help, we qualify for grace.

Jesus was compassionate toward Peter and had faith in him. Although Peter may not have felt that he had unqualified love, Christ looked beyond the now and told him prophetically that he would one day lay down his life and walk in unconditional love. History records that when martyrdom came knocking, Peter preferred to be crucified upside down; he did not think he was worthy to be crucified like his Master. What a transformation! Still, Peter's change was progressive.

On the day of Pentecost, Peter demonstrated boldness. He spoke up, risking arrest, and three thousand were saved. When they were arrested after the healing of the blind man at the beautiful gate and were warned not to preach again in the name of Jesus, Peter spoke up and asked whether it was better to obey God rather than man. When Herod arrested Peter and was ready to execute him, the night before the execution Peter slept soundly and had to be awakened by an angel. The old, unbroken Peter would probably have negotiated a deal with the establishment or planned on a jail break. But he was unperturbed. He had died to his own ways and his own agenda. Peter was living for the Lord. He understood that he was bought with a price, and could only live for the Lord. The old Peter had learned how to die in order for the glory of God to be seen. It had been a process in Peter's life.[11]

PAUL

The apostle Paul was born with the name Saul at Tarsus in Cilicia. He had inherited the privileges of a Roman citizen from his father. He studied in Jerusalem under Gamaliel, the most distinguished rabbi of his day. He also learned the art of tent-making to complement his formal education. (See Acts 18:3; 20:34; 2 Thessalonians 3:8.) He was learned in the Law, a strict Pharisee, a defender of Judaism, and a bitter enemy of Christianity. He was part of the Sanhedrin forces with special authority to imprison Christians. (See Acts 9:2.) Saul was a blasphemer, someone who showed no respect to others, a cocky person who was not afraid to ridicule other people. Persecuting and injurious, he enjoyed making other people's lives difficult. He was present at the stoning of Stephen. He consented to it; he was in full agreement. He enjoyed injuring others. It gave him a thrill as stones landed and houses were burnt. He enjoyed seeing the blood spilling out of Stephen's wounds. He not only kept the garments of the accusers, but also cheered those who carried out this assignment. He would later become the most feared persecutor of the church, taking the torture of the saints to another level. The prayers of love, the conviction and devotion of Stephen, and the glory of God that shone on his face were an eternal seed planted in the heart of Saul.[12]

On the way to Damascus, Saul had a divine encounter with the Lord. He was blinded by light, and the Lord Jesus personally spoke to him. He surrendered. There, God gave him a new name: Paul.

Paul came to Jesus in a powerful way. He had very high credentials and would have been a danger to himself and the kingdom without spiritual brokenness, but he realized that his natural credentials were not what put him in the ministry; it was the mercy of God and the dealings of God that put him in the ministry. He realized that big in the world does not mean big in the church.

It is important to remember Paul's background, because getting saved is not necessarily evidence that you have been broken, and are ready to be fruitful. The potential is there, but the process must begin.

Paul was arguably the most notorious persecutor of the church in his time, and he was convinced that his activities against the church were a duty to God. However, when he encountered the Lord, he showed great passion for the work of the ministry and the testimony of the Lord. Almost immediately after his salvation, Paul began to preach in the synagogues, and the Jews sought to kill him day and night. The disciples lowered him down the city wall in a basket to help him escape, and he headed for Jerusalem.

In Jerusalem the disciples would not receive Paul because of his notorious reputation, but a divine appointment with Barnabas opened the door. He became bolder and disputed with the Grecians, and they plotted to kill him. The apostles decided to send Paul back to his hometown, and the Word says the churches had rest and multiplied after Paul's exit.[13]

Naturally speaking, Paul was the biggest catch the church had at this time. In today's world, his testimony in Christian media would have made headlines. Someone might have hurriedly given him ordination papers.

It is sad that when celebrities get saved, people try to make them celebrities in the church. The church is a place for sons and servants. Sometimes people who have no calling are put in the fivefold ministry. If there is no oil from God on their heads, it does not matter who lays hands on them; if they are not called by God, the laying on of hands cannot call them.

A person who is called to the ministry of helps may be thrust into the ministry if he is wealthy or a person of means. The thinking that governs this ungodly practice is that he would use his resources to serve God. There is an epidemic of hirelings, people with no calling, running ministries. If a man must be put at the helm of affairs or ordained as a pastor before he supports the gospel, he does not even qualify for the ministry of helps, much less the fivefold ministry.

There is supernatural equipment for the offices of ministry. God's anointing comes on the person who is called, and he has a supernatural ability to function. There are so many pastors who are supposed to be deacons and function in the ministry of help. Stephen was a deacon before the Lord promoted him. Every believer is called to the ministry of reconciliation, and as an ambassador for the kingdom, everywhere we go, be it an office or a school, becomes our "pulpit."

WILDERNESS

Paul was called, but he was not broken. He needed to go to God's Bible school. After Paul returned to Tarsus, we do not hear about him for a long time. Scholars have suggested that this was the time he went into Arabia. He was in the wilderness, where he was personally taught by the Lord for three years. Paul returned from the school of the wilderness. Imagine having no contact with established Christianity, waiting before the Lord, for three years.

We are reminded of Moses, who fought so hard to manifest

his calling. He killed a man in the process and was forced to the backside of the desert for forty years to tend his father-in-law's sheep. There God showed his ways unto Moses. In Moses, God was building the character he needed to lead His people. He was taking away so much of his personal ambition, that when God called him to go back to Egypt, there were no personal motives involved.

Paul was led much like Moses. The school in the wilderness is a place of brokenness where we learn the ways of God. Paul learned the heart of God because by experience he had learned to lay down his own goals and way of doing things to surrender to God's higher order. The apostle spent those valuable years in the wilderness where God was dealing with things in his flesh. Some of the revelations he received and wrote in his epistles were received at this time.

Upon his return he expected to be launched into ministry, but it seemed the apostles had forgotten him. Paul had great credentials—his academic qualifications, his celebrity status, his conversion, his time in Arabia during which he was personally taught by the Lord—but God and the church seemed to put him on the shelf, or so it seemed.

Reports had been received in Jerusalem about the expansion of the gospel amongst the Gentiles and elsewhere as the saints had scattered through persecution. Barnabas was selected to go as far as Antioch to follow up on these developments. He literally had to hunt for Paul; it appears he had to go up and down trying to locate him. The verb used here to describe Barnabas's search for Paul is the same verb used when Jesus's parents were seeking him after they left him behind in the temple. (See Luke 2:44–45, "to seek up and down, back and forth, to hunt up, to make a thorough search till success comes.")[14]

> Then departed Barnabas to Tarsus, for to seek Saul: And when he had found him, he brought him unto Antioch. And it came to pass, that a whole year they assembled themselves with the church, and taught much people. And the disciples were called Christians first in Antioch.
>
> —Acts 11:25–26

Paul did not come to Antioch as a superstar. He worked under Barnabas, and they established the believers. It was in Antioch that believers were first called Christians. Paul was well learned, fluent in Greek with a deep Hebrew theological background, yet he was just one of the ministers under the wings of Barnabas. When Agabus came from Jerusalem to Antioch and prophesied about the impending famine, it was Paul who was chosen to help Barnabas distribute the relief to the brethren in Judea.[15]

Paul realized that it was not his natural credentials that put him in the ministry. He had gone up to Jerusalem and was sent home by the apostles. He had been silent for years, and were it not for God working through Barnabas to bring him to Antioch, he realized he might still have been in obscurity. The silent years were part of God's design to deepen his character and his message.

Paul stayed faithful in Antioch and was listed in the thirteenth chapter of Acts among the prophets and teachers who were waiting on the Lord. Finally, the Lord spoke, and he was released under the leadership of Barnabas for the apostolic ministry.

Paul learned that the most important goal is to allow the refining fire of Christ to remove all the impurities from our lives, so we reflect only the glory of God. In order for this to happen, God removes all the fleshly glories. He allows pressure to come to us and puts us through the fire. As he grades us, He determines what level of use He can put us through.[16] Some of God's metals jump out of the fire and limit themselves. But God grades, refines, and chooses us as we pass the test the same way a refiner's fire exposes the quality of the product.

Why did Paul need such training and preparation? Because the foundation of the building is very important; the higher the building, the deeper the foundation must go. Ministry essentially flows from our lives, and a shallow foundation cannot support a strong building with great height. It takes a longer time to build the foundation of a strong house.

The apostle Paul went on to lead a life of active ministry because God built a foundation of brokenness in his life. Paul's journey was progressive, as seen in his writings. At the beginning he felt he was equal with the other apostles, then least of the apostles, least of all saints, and toward the end he felt he was the chief of sinners. Brokenness in the life of Paul is demonstrated in the fact that he decreased in his own estimation, and he allowed the grace of God to be manifested in his life. Brokenness is that process that allows the works of the flesh in the outer man to be put to death daily.

Then as the outer shell decays, the inward man, which is created in the likeness of Christ, can be seen. John the Baptist echoed the same truth, that we must decrease and Jesus must increase.

Paul realized that he could not make it in the ministry by means of natural credentials.[17] God had to deliver him from attitudes and mind-sets from past years. The Lord tried his heart for years before he found him faithful in the ministry. Why the long wait? Good wine, they say, is poured slowly. God takes time to train and try our hearts. What we consider our priorities and star qualities need to be refined and sometimes destroyed. If we hang on to selfish dreams and human ego, He needs to put us back in the flame like the refiner of silver has to do until he sees his image in the silver. This process is not only true for ministers but for every believer. God wants us to be conformed to the image of his son. This type of suffering allows the character of God to be developed.

I remember flying back home from a mission trip when the Lord spoke audibly to me. He said, "You have passed another test." My wife and I had been invited to minister in another nation. On arrival we learned quickly that there was no food to eat, and the minister was going through a lean period. We had to feed ourselves and the pastor's family. Accommodations were woeful, with a pit toilet right in front of our room. I felt like teaching him about how to be hospitable, but the Lord told me to be quiet. We visited another work of theirs in a neighboring country and had to cover the cost ourselves with no prior discussion. Again, I felt like teaching him about responsibility.

We left with a handshake and obviously without any honorarium. I wanted to show him the scripture about a laborer being worthy of his hire, but the Lord said it was not my business. We stayed cheerful and had a good attitude, and God moved with many miracles. When the Lord spoke those words to me on the plane trip home, it was more than a reward. Within three months God opened ministry and financial doors to my wife and I that were beyond our imagination.

Every believer will experience difficult people, those who do not appreciate our efforts or people who are just plain nasty. We should pray for God to deliver us from such people. God may not take you out of that situation, but instead He may allow you to develop the fruit of the Spirit through the challenges. Stamina and experience are developed when we overcome challenges and trials.

A person who fails to pass elementary courses should not be allowed to take advanced courses, because the next program is based on what was learned before. Samuel was weaned before his mother brought him to the prophet Eli at Shiloh. Had he not been weaned, he would have become a liability. In life and ministry, jumping the process produces half-done, ill-equipped ministers. When some jump the process and advance, they may believe they are OK, but in God's book they needed to have repeated the test. What is the yardstick of real success? It is going through God's process of brokenness and refusing to be moved by human commendation or censure.

Some things we celebrate as successes may be an abomination

before God. It may smell, look, taste, and feel like God, but may not be of God. Things of God must have His trademark. They have been through the Refiner's fire, and they manifest the fruit of the Spirit.[18]

In today's microwave age things happen really fast, and the sign of fruitfulness for some is how fast you achieve, not how thorough you build. The admonition to run the race with patience is often overlooked. The ideal believer to some is one who succeeds in the shortest possible time. The best church is the one built in the shortest time with the largest number of followers. But Paul warns us to be careful how we build; human character cannot be molded in the microwave. God pays attention to every area, and His timing is critical. God is interested in how thoroughly you build, and if you have kept the rules of engagement.

Believers may go through periods of isolation and rejection in order for God to deliver them from the opinions and praise of men. God's process of refining our character through the Word and divine encounters is not the most palatable. Moses had to spend forty years preparing for his ministry. He reached a point where he was delivered from his private agenda in order to pursue God's agenda. He had to work and submit to Jethro, but God compensated him with more glory and power than what he left in Egypt. He was not mindful of what he left behind; it became to him as nothing compared to what God would present to him after he had been broken by the Lord.

EARLY FIRES

I remember as a young undergraduate when we had a revival on campus that brought the hardest, most unbelieving cult students into the fold of Christ. Although I did not have any plans to start a new fellowship, the doors of leading Christian groups were not opened to these unchurched people. The Lord spoke to me, instructing me to begin to teach and assemble them into a fellowship group. This began a revival, and no two meetings were the same in those early days. The new believers were so hungry for God and worshiped with so much passion and intimacy that the tangible presence of God was there every time we met. Healings, singing in the spirit, being slain in the spirit, prophecies, gifts of the spirit, and other manifestations of the spirit were commonplace.

Many souls were won, especially amongst people without a church background, but the fire of persecution was enormous. The style of dressing of many of these unchurched people was very offensive to older Christians in the body. The young Christians were loud and very exuberant in their new-found faith, and some were out-rightly rejected. For opening the doors of the fellowship to these people, I was excommunicated. Major Christian groups called us heretics and backslidden. Some even called us a cult.

That work is still going on today after twenty five years. Thousands of students have been saved and have graduated, and are a major blessing to the body of Christ because of it. As the leader of this movement, it is interesting to look back and see how the move of God at that time has helped to bring many other sister groups into balance over the years. Our new group made mistakes, but in spite of that, God still worked out His purposes.

A great work was done in me. I learned, among other things, how to stand alone, how to be focused in the middle of a deluge of criticisms, and how to seek God in prayer. I cried many tears because of rejection. All along the Lord was saying to me, "Get over it. They are not going to change you, and it won't hurt you." This was only the beginning of a series of fires that came to purify my life at an early age.

Difficult situations come and go, but each trial helps to prepare us for the next one. Every level has a new devil, and the ones you fail to defeat at your last post are waiting with others in the new level. The challenges we go through help to build stamina for the next level. Jesus suffered when cruel remarks were made about His background. Those who derided him questioned His authority and might have questioned his paternity. He was rejected outright by people in His hometown, but He set aside His glory to become a man. He was so settled that He was not moved by the jeers, not even during His final suffering on the cross. He had chosen to obey God, to set aside any other agenda and glorify God.

Suffering persecution and training in character is not comfortable, but to manifest the fruit of the Spirit is a process. Thank God for His gifts; they are manifested by the Lord through us to bless others. We serve as channels and conduits for those divine graces, but growing fruits in our lives requires brokenness. Gifts are not a badge of spiritual maturity, but the fruits are the products of God's dealing in our lives. They are the litmus test, the real indicator, of where we are in Christ.[19]

Kenneth Hagin, in his book *Must Christians Suffer?* shares some insight:

> People want to accuse the devil of getting them into the wilderness. But Jesus was led by the Spirit into the wilderness to be tempted of the devil. The Spirit led Him. That's what the Bible means when it says, "He was perfected through the things He suffered." Whether you realize it or not, these are the things that are going to make us or break us.
>
> Here's where faith comes in, and here's where the tragedy is.
>
> People, listening to faith teachers, get the idea that they are going to sail through life and that everything is going to be "hunky dory." They think they'll never have trials, tests or suffering of any kind. Then somebody rises up and says something about them and they're ready to quit.
>
> You're going to have persecution. Jesus said in John 16:33, "These things I have spoken unto you, that in me ye might have peace. In the world ye shall have tribulation: but be of good cheer; I have overcome the world."
>
> My ministry wouldn't be what it is today if I hadn't pastored that first church. And it wouldn't be what it is if I hadn't pastored my last church. Some of the hardest tests I have gone through in 50 years of experience are because I was led by the Spirit of

God. He knew the test was coming. It was God's way of teaching me.

You can't learn some things just by reading the written Word. It's when you put the Word into practice that it becomes real to you.[20]

3

CHAMPION-TURNED-VILLAIN

AVID WAS A shepherd boy who did not seek the throne, but the throne found him. The prophet Samuel had been directed by the Lord to anoint another king in the place of backslidden Saul. The house of Jesse was the place from which the future king would emerge. Upon reaching Jesse's house, his sons were summoned, but David was not included in the number. His father did not think the young David qualified, but the ceremony could not proceed without him, as the Lord rejected all the older sons called by Jesse. David was summoned from the fields, and was promptly confirmed as the Lord's choice. He was anointed but returned to the pasture where he had his assignment hitherto.

The anointing of God is not an indication of a ministry launch. On the contrary, it is a signal for intensive training, brokenness, and preparation for what lies ahead. Every phase of our walk with the Lord requires new training. The Father is the one who determines when we are ready for the next level as we yield to the dealings of the Holy Spirit in our lives.

David the Giant-Slayer-Turned-Villain

David met Goliath by divine appointment. He had no scheme or plan to become famous by killing Goliath. His father had requested that he carry supplies to his brothers, who were in the battlefront. Upon his approach he heard the blasphemy of Goliath and wondered why the army allowed such dishonor against the Lord to go unchallenged. He saw no difference between this giant and the lion and the bear he had wrestled and killed when he kept his father's sheep. He knew God had helped him to overcome these wild animals, because as an Israelite he understood that he bore the mark of circumcision, a confirmation that he was in covenant with the almighty God, who would back him up in any conflict.

He decided to take on Goliath, much to the chagrin of his brothers. King Saul allowed young David to face Goliath, but only after David had turned down the king's armor and restated his credentials from past victories. He came out of the contest victorious, cutting off the head of Goliath. David's secret preparation paid off when divine opportunity arose. Smith Wigglesworth said, "You must live ready at all times."[1] When divine appointment arrives, the believer must be ready. Many miss out because they practice seasonal commitment and convenient obedience. In the workplace a committed and conscientious professional has to be consistently excellent, because you cannot tell when the big client will come in. To be unprepared when your opportunity comes is to miss the moment of visitation.[2]

David must have been a great young man before his victory over Goliath made him famous; how else could we explain the integrity and courage he demonstrated rescuing the family sheep from the mouths of lion and bear? He showed greatness when he went beyond the call of duty to put his life at risk for the sheep. These were some of the traits that endeared him to the Lord before he was chosen as king. A person may be famous but not great. Greatness comes from the selfless things we do for others. A person can be famous for his achievements, but it may be personal gain and have no bearing upon other people's lives. Jesus said to be great we must serve others.[3] David was great before he became famous. He was already making unbelievable sacrifices before God promoted him.

No sooner had David won the famous victory than the king assigned him to serve him. He maintained faithfulness as always. He had built a lifestyle of excellence when he worked for his father. David carried out his assignment with integrity, but the songs of the women who sang about David killing ten thousand and Saul killing a thousand remained such an indelible refrain in Saul's mind that he envied David and wanted him dead.

THE SIZE OF YOUR OPPOSITION IS AN INDICATION OF THE SIZE OF DESTINY

David had conquered Goliath, an unusual feat for a teenager, but he must now face the wrath of his own king. His travail came after he was anointed king and experienced his famous victory against Goliath. The songs of the women did nothing to David, because he remained levelheaded and committed to his king. He attributed his success to God. On a real team it is not important whose name is famous, but that the job gets done and the glory goes to the Lord.

David and Jonathan, Saul's son, were knit together in their hearts, and they cut a covenant, which was a key to David's survival. The king wanted David dead. Jonathan confirmed to David the evil plot of the king. The king's offer of his daughter, Michal, to David for a hundred foreskins of the Philistines was to make her a snare to him and to see David perish in the hands of the Philistines. But David, true to type, went beyond what was required and brought two hundred foreskins from Philistines. Michal helped David plan an escape, and so began David's journey as a fugitive. He was anointed. He had committed no sin but was led into the wilderness to be tempted and tested like the Lord Jesus was before His ministry was released.

GOD SHAKES YOUR WORLD TO SHAPE YOUR DESTINY

How quickly things can change. Just as David the hero had become the villain, many of the people who had once followed Jesus turned on him. The same people that said, "Hosanna!"

when He entered Jerusalem were crying, "Crucify Him!" a few days later. A believer's self-esteem cannot be measured by the praise and the approval of men. Neither can it be measured by material acquisition, because wealth can take wings and fly away. God warned us about trusting in uncertain riches. Anything other than God is temporary. One moment of indiscretion can ruin an entire life or ministry.

God will sometimes remove the things or persons we have put our confidence in. He may have us bring our "Isaac," like Abraham, or run away from our dreams, like Moses when he had to run from Egypt. These wilderness experiences are the process of brokenness, when God strips us of worldly strategies and ways of doing things. David was a hero but was forced to live as a fugitive. He was anointed king but had no throne or domain. He had to wander until the time established by the Father. Galatians 4:1–2 declares that the heir is put under tutors and governors until he matures to take the throne.[4] Through his travails, there were times David wondered what he had done to attract all these troubles. God was purifying him, helping him to examine his motives. Was he kingdom-motivated or self-motivated?

David faced challenges beyond his years. He faced Goliath when his older brothers, the army commandants, and the king were terrified. He had unusual enemies and competition from unlikely sources, such as the king, who became envious of him. This was an indication of the size of his destiny. His foundations had to be rooted in God. God has a great destiny for all His children, and while the benefits of salvation are all ours now, the character to sustain us as we walk in those blessings must be built through a process that requires brokenness and patience. Jesus taught that one of the reasons faith can fail to produce is unforgiveness, but for some believers that is the last area they look at when things are not working. (For example, there are couples worshiping in church but struggling with unforgiveness in the bedroom.)

In the wilderness God reduces you to increase you. Every believer's heart will be tried before God moves him into the fullness of his purpose. True, all the benefits of redemption are ours now—forgiveness of sin, healing and health, preservation and protection, blessings and prosperity—but the fruit of the Spirit must be manifest if we will walk in the fuller measures of these blessings.

Jesus walked in the fullness of His covenant, but His life made an impact as He laid it down daily for others. As I said before, financial blessings are like manure: spread them around, and they are a blessing and source of thanksgiving to God, as you can transform people's lives. But heap it on yourself, and it stinks. Christlikeness is God's desire for us as we appropriate every blessing that Jesus purchased on the cross. God wants us to have all that Jesus purchased, with the stamp of godliness written all over us.

Abraham was blessed, but his turning point came when he laid down his blessing on the altar and was ready to kill Isaac. God released him into his purpose, which was to bless the whole of humanity. God stopped Abraham from killing his own son, but put His own Son, Jesus, on the cross so that through Abraham He could be a blessing to the whole world.

Abraham laid down his best. He was broken. He died to his own agenda, and God fulfilled the greater purposes.

Sometimes people start in the Word and the Spirit but end up in the flesh because they stop dying daily like Paul taught. Their witness is cut short. They may still profess their faith but are not on the cutting edge of what God is doing. God wanted Abraham to put his best seed on the altar so that he would have the opportunity to put Jesus on the cross.[5]

When God allows your world to be shaken you are initiated into the school of the Holy Spirit. Here was David, whose praises the women sang. Here was David, son-in-law to the king; a man promoted to work with the king. Suddenly his world was shaken, and nothing was sure anymore. The women who sang his praise were gone. The armies of Israel who were saved by his bravery were no longer there to extol his prowess. His parents could not help him. His brothers probably felt that David was the architect of his own downfall. Had he stayed with the flock and listened to their counsel he would not have fought Goliath, and landed himself in this strange situation.

In the school of the Spirit, God removes your props. You burn your bridges, come as you are, and you are trained to survive in the battle by the help of God alone. It is similar to a woman in the pangs of labor. The husband and friends may be telling her they are with her, but there is no way she can have natural birth without going through the pain. She must go through the actual experience alone. She could write a book after the experience of childbirth is over describing her agony and triumph, but those who read her story must have their own experience before they can have their own testimony. We may read the Word of God, but until we apply the Word in the times of trials, we cannot call it our own.

Believers must be wary of the spirit of mammon and the world's way of doing things. In the world success is judged by size, income, spread, profit margin, assets, and other material and carnal indices. God has a different set of rules. Philip completed a great evangelistic campaign in Samaria, and the Spirit led him to join the Ethiopian eunuch's chariot. He went from a multitude to one person. In the world that is a declining fortune, but God was seeing the gospel going to an entire continent. Some believers and ministers alike may choose not to serve or minister in certain places if they are considered below their target audience or their level, but Jesus went everywhere the Spirit led Him and touched lives.

Believers need to die to their flesh and personal ego. Jesus did not die to make you a superstar. It is important that our costs are covered and we spend wisely, but I have ministered in many places (and still do) where I receive nothing. Then in another place God compensates and more than covers the cost. The practice of non-refundable deposits by itinerant ministers is a worldly practice. You are ministering based on a financial arrangement. The deposit is to guarantee that costs are covered, should the host fail to meet the budget. It is rather more important to seek God about where He wants you to go. This has led to oversaturation. While in many places very little has been done and ministers are scarce, in other places churches are competing for places. Who pays you, man or God?

The spirit of mammon only judges you by how much you have and how big you are. The kingdom operates in the opposite direction; we are to strengthen the weak. We are blessed to be a blessing. The test of Abraham was of an extreme nature. The purpose of God was to ensure that no possession stood between him and Abraham. God required total commitment from Abraham. Of all his possessions, Isaac was the symbolic representation of his life, a child of his old age, the laughter in his home, Sarah's joy and dignity, the seed for his future and lineage. But God wanted him to commit Isaac into His hands and let go of him.

Jesus said the things would be added unto us; Jesus did not say things would be glued to us.[6] Material things must remain things. They must not be more important than God or become so big we cannot give them away. Have you noticed that no one dies and takes any material thing away? That is because we do not own them, because the earth is the Lord's. We use these things and leave them to others.

The more God elevates us, the more we are to humble ourselves under His hand. More blessings mean more responsibility to walk humbly before the Lord. Our money must have assignments; otherwise, it becomes a golden calf. Israel's gold became their idol in the wilderness. Money without purpose and integrity can make believers egotistical and vain, like the unsaved. When we embrace brokenness and surrender, nothing in this world can be more important than our relationship with the Lord. We see the Lord, and every other thing becomes like dung.

Where was David's honor in the wilderness? Where were

Paul's credentials in the wilderness? Where were Jacob's bravery and wit when he wept before the Lord at Jabbok? Where were Peter's assertiveness and boldness when he denied Jesus? God does not want us putting our faith in anything or anyone but Him. This must be stripped before God can move us to our next level and to wealthy places. It is quite possible to skip the school of brokenness, lean on your wit, and still make progress, but it would lack the hallmark of heaven. It would be hollow and your impact limited.

Impact is about changed lives. On Mount Carmel the prophet of Baal made a lot of noise. His priests were spectacular in their displays, but there was no response from heaven. Their colorful displays did not bring anyone close to God. There were many spectators who enjoyed their entertainment. Church life also sometimes tries to mimic the world, but we are not called to copy or compete with the world. Those who truly encounter the Lord have acquired a divine taste to which nothing in this world compares; they are satisfied only with what is genuine. When Elijah prayed to God on Mount Carmel, He answered, and there was repentance.

You can learn the theory about surviving in the wilderness in Bible school, but you can only truly survive when you depend on your Instructor, your Teacher, the Holy Spirit, in the wilderness. Jesus was led into the wilderness to be tempted of the devil. The Holy Spirit guided Him and brought Him through. The Word of God was exalted in the face of each challenge. The wilderness is a place where you must dig your own well, like Isaac had to re-dig. Like Moses, you may need to find your burning bush. Wrestle with the angel and limp off as Jacob did. Lay your Isaac on the altar like Abraham. Be strengthened like the Lord Jesus was in the wilderness.

The brokenness required for each person's progression depends on the assignment and the vessel. For example, David had developed a shepherd's heart and conquered the lion, the bear, and Goliath. Now he needed to learn how to deal with rejection, how to train and raise men, how to conquer and subdue all nations around him, and much more.

There are challenges you go through with the devil breathing down your neck, and although many may stand around you, you feel alone and vulnerable. David was forced to seek God by himself. He was going to begin his life as a fugitive. When Jesus went into the wilderness, He also went alone. When Jesus had fasted, the flesh was weak, and Satan took advantage of that fact to pile his pressure on Him. But Jesus leaned on the Word and the Spirit. In times like these when there seems to be no one to talk to, and the pressures are mounting, deep must call unto deep. You cannot talk about the wells that Abraham dug, which Isaac later inherited. You must find your own water, seek your own consecration, climb your own mountain, wrestle with your own angel and devils—but God will be there, and His Word will stand by you.

I am reminded of an usher in our church whose daughter was miraculously raised from the dead. He and his wife knew from the ultrasound that their baby was dead from the womb, but his wife's bleeding was life threatening. Doctors fought and were able to save her life, but the baby was dead on arrival, as they had feared. He decided to wrestle in prayer and refuse the sentence of death. After a while, the baby came back to life. He fought. He had a testimony. He was about to lose two people at once, but his faith, though severely tested, was victorious.

4

NAVIGATING WILDERNESS EXPERIENCES

SAUL'S GOAL
1 SAMUEL 19:18–24[1]

THE CHALLENGES DAVID faced after defeating Goliath and falling out of favor with King Saul were of great proportion. King Saul sought to kill him. David escaped through a carefully knit plot by Michal, his wife, who was Saul's daughter. Finding the ancient landmarks and a mentor were of the utmost importance to David, a man who would nurture the pure stream of God in him. There must be father figures and spiritual landmarks where the believer and minister must rest and get his bearings. David sought the prophet Samuel, the man who anointed him as king. What better place than in Naioth in Ramah, which was a school of prophets?

It is true that in your isolation the Holy Spirit is your Teacher and Helper, but there are spiritual guides God has placed in your path. You will have to walk through your fire alone, but mentors are valuable for counsel, prayer, and guidance. No person arrives at the place of destiny alone. There are guides. Moses was the guide for Israel. Moses had Jethro as a mentor, David had Samuel, Paul had Barnabas, and Timothy had Paul, to mention a few. A man without a mentor is bound to repeat the mistakes of history.

When Saul heard that David was with Samuel, he sent three sets of messengers to capture David. They were all delayed before the Lord and prophesied. Saul came, and he prophesied and stripped himself naked. This is interesting, as Saul's goal was evil, and he was backslidden. Yet, the anointing came on him. The anointing upon an individual is not necessarily a sign of approval or spirituality. After all, Balaam's donkey prophesied. Fruits are not like the plastic gifts on the Christmas tree used for our decoration. They are not edible, but they are good to look at. Real fruit must be borne by the seed dying and bringing out new life through a process; only then can our lives have impact. Saul prophesying was not a sign of approval; the Lord seemed to have used the anointing to hold Saul down so David could escape.

RENEWING COVENANT TIES
1 SAMUEL 20:1–4²

Jesus is described in Scripture as a friend that sticks closer than a brother. When the people we feel closest to naturally fail us, He is always there. Jonathan acted the same way on David's behalf. Jonathan was kingdom-minded and was able to discern the hand of God on David. Therefore, he honored the covenant and helped to establish the plan of God among men. As David and Jonathan reunited, Jonathan reassured him that he would defend him before King Saul, and would make sure that no harm came to him. Jonathan had taken a stand against his father and promised to reveal Saul's wicked plans to David.

Every ministry needs covenant men who are willing to sacrifice natural ties for the covenant we have in Christ. Ministries and churches sometimes face division because people are not willing to rise above their family, political, ethnic, social, or professional ties when matters of the kingdom are involved. It is not about what political parties we belong to; it is about what is right for the kingdom of God. Jonathan showed that he believed there is only one kingdom; the one the Lord approves of. The person following the blueprint of heaven is the leader irrespective of his tribe, location, or race. Ministries fail to reach their full potential because the "Jonathans" sent by God sometimes compromise.

Satan always seeks to destroy the anointed. How else might we come to terms with the demonic, rabid obsession of King Saul to destroy the young man who helped to save his kingdom from the Philistines? This was nothing more than

Satan's agenda to annihilate David and destroy the purposes of God. The attacks that come against servants of God and believers may look ordinary, but beneath this is the master stroke of the enemy to abort destinies.

Satan wanted Moses removed at infancy. He was born out of season, when male children were fed to crocodiles, yet God preserved him. At age two he was supposed to be dead, and at eighty years old he became Israel's deliverer. The enemy is a strategist, but God is always ahead of him.

The Lord Jesus was to be killed at infancy. Satan entered Herod when he heard from the wise men when they saw the star at Jesus's birth. He proceeded to snuff out the lives of many children under the age of two, because Satan knew that Jesus had come to destroy his works.

Staying Close to the Streams of God
2 Samuel 21:1–9[3]

David escaped to Nob, the place of wandering. In his uncertain existence he strove to stay close to the godly. He sought out the high priest, who allowed him to eat the holy bread. This could be likened to feeding on the Word of God and staying around godly people.

If we follow the conversation between David and Ahimelech, the high priest, we see that Ahimelech asked David genuine questions about how cleanly David and his men had lived before he gave him the holy bread. This is a genuine mentoring relationship in which real questions were asked. Ministers sometimes avoid mentors who ask the tough questions about their marriage, money issues, immorality, and the like. Spiritual leaders who avoid discussing the real issues can be guilty of contributory negligence. Eli rebuked his sons ever so softly, and he lost both his ministry and his sons. God has not called anyone in the body of Christ to police the church, but when people put themselves under a leader for oversight, that leader assumes a responsibility. With some ministers, you can get away with anything once you give them large personal offerings. These sound more like hirelings than leaders with integrity.

Ahimelech gave the sword of Goliath to David that day, confirming to him that the victory of yesterday was no fluke. He was encouraging him that what God did before, He would do again. Goliath's sword must have become a living memorial for David as he continued to fight the battle of his life.

David, however, was not sincere with Ahimelech, and the Scriptures do not conceal this. He was a work in progress. Fear was the reason behind the lie David told. He suggested that the king had sent him on an errand he could not disclose. This lie eventually led to the death of Ahimelech; Doeg the Edomite reported seeing him and David together, Ahimelech and the other priests paid the supreme price. Had David told the truth, that he was a fugitive, maybe Ahimelech's approach would have been different; this event must have weighed on heavily on David's heart when he asked the Lord to deliver him from lying.[4]

David tried to stay true to the streams of God, seeking out Samuel and Ahimelech, but the pressure and chase of Saul meant that those relationships were threatened. He could not be within the physical proximity of these anointed men. God was using these challenges to get David to dig his own spiritual well, to climb his own rock of intimacy. There may come a time when your spiritual parents and mentors may not be physically accessible, and you must divide the Jordan yourself. Elisha had to do it, and with the strength of the Lord, you can do the same.

SURVIVAL SKILLS

David escaped to Gath, the wine press. He faked insanity before King Achish in order to survive. He is believed to have written Psalm 34 at this time, the contents of which further reveal the trauma he was going through. A wine press, as the name suggests, is the place where juice is squeezed out of the grapes. When the pressure of the moment causes a king to scribble on the door and allow his spittle to run down his beard in order to disguise his true identity, then he is at the bottom, where ego and personal achievements mean nothing.

David had to put up this show with his lieutenants watching him. They had seen and heard of "David who killed Goliath, a great warrior," but before their eyes they saw a man desperate for life. There was no dignity in David at this point: a giant slayer, a man of war, a man whose place was already assured in the folklore of Israel now drooling and feigning insanity? This was most inappropriate, but God was showing David that true greatness was only in Him, as any earthly achievement is temporary.

David's humanity did not take away from his greatness, so the soldiers continued to follow him. Genuine disciples do not reject or despise their mentors or leaders because they exhibit human frailties. David just lied to the priest and at the next stop. He feigned insanity, but although his actions were not noble, his followers knew his heart.

Is it not amusing that today you may be celebrated, and in the next breath someone else may take you to the cleaners and demean you, while you do not even have control over their words? Maybe God is helping to give us a clear perspective about how we see ourselves. Believers should be dead to censure or praise and alive only to the Father's approval.

KING OF THE CAVE DWELLERS: ADULLAM
1 SAMUEL 22:1–2[5]

David escaped to Adullam, a cave which was located in a valley, and all the distressed, discontented, and indebted people showed up. The cave was not where he was anointed to be as a king. David rose above his place in the cave to minister to others. It was indeed a great testimony that David raised mighty men of valor out of rejects and nobodies. It was a testimony, because everyone who came needed him, and he needed God.

It must have been lonely ministering to all these people while he was running for his life. Many times in the ministry those who minister to others are forgotten. People are oblivious of the fact that the ministers have to face their own challenges. Pastors help to dry the tears of others, but must find strength in God to encourage themselves. Adullam is a statement about God's grace, which can bring transformation in the life of the most disadvantaged person. Don't despise the cave-dwellers who walk into your church. They may be broke and sick, but even the best piece of furniture existed as an ordinary tree until somebody saw its potential.

David did not have the cream of the crop of society rooting for him, but his leadership was accepted and celebrated. God was giving him a pulpit in the cave to prepare for a dais in the palace. The cave was a rehearsal for the palace. Some people fail to treat their cave assignments with the seriousness and devotion they require, and as such God is unable to trust them with the responsibilities of the palace.

Moab
1 Samuel 22:3–5[6]

The anointing does not remove your family responsibilities. David feared what Saul might do to his family; in his desperation he could use them as hostages to get David to show himself, or he could just massacre them. David was open to the voice of God. The prophet Gad brought a word that he should not stay in the hold but go into the land of Judah.

David proceeded to Hareth, and the news of his presence brought out the worst in Saul. Saul appealed to his clan, the Benjamites, from whom David was perceived to want to take the throne. Saul accused them of disloyalty. He wanted their support, even if he was wrong.

As the tirade of accusations mounted, Doeg the Edomite, who had seen David with Ahimelech, the priest, recounted the incident. Ahimelech was put to death alongside eighty-five other priests because he fed David. This action of Saul demonstrates the extreme measures people who seek power are willing to take to stay in control. When power, not service, becomes the ultimate goal, ministries can operate like mafia outfits, where anything can be done for power. It is ungodly. Saul was about his empire, not the kingdom.

The contrast between Abraham's attitude toward Lot when there was strife between them is in sharp contrast to Saul's insane quest to hold on to power and destroy his perceived opponents. Abraham knew who called him, and he refused to be in competition with his nephew. When leaders focus on building the kingdom, making Jesus known and pleasing Him are their goals; but leaders who focus on themselves build their Towers of Babel to make a name for their empires. A house not built by the Lord can only be sustained by the arm of flesh. Nothing that we build for our own glory could stand the test of time. The one who is building a name or an empire is responsible for protecting his empire, and such persons are man-made; they live under intolerable stress.

Loyalty and Betrayal: Keliah
1 Samuel 23:1–13[7]

Saul was seeking to kill David, as he felt he was trapped in Keliah. David inquired of the Lord through Abiathar, the priest, who confirmed his premonition and fears. Saul would come after him, and the people he had delivered from the Philistines in God's name would betray him to Saul. Repaying evil for good is exactly what the people of Keliah planned to do, but this is an unfortunate reality of life that every believer and minister needs to accept. The Bible teaches that we are not to render evil for evil or get even when people despitefully use us. This requires putting the flesh under daily, and spiritual brokenness in the believer's life.[8]

What is your reaction when people to whom you have been a blessing turn against you? Are you bitter, or do you bless them and move on? In human relationships, these occurrences are commonplace. There is no point hanging on to something in your life that was an accident. An accident in your life needs not become the story of your life. Unforgiveness will make you a prisoner of your past. The past must be allowed to go, and betrayal must be forgiven. It may be hard to forgive, but it is the only way to a healthy life.

I have listened to many people's personal stories, and sometimes I wonder within myself if I could go through what they have suffered and survive. The truth is, the people who have been so afflicted never thought they could survive prior to the challenge; God gives us enough grace for each encounter. Forgiving those who offend and hurt us is part of brokenness, because sometimes you must overcome feeling that you are justified in your longing for revenge.

WILDERNESS OF ZIPH: FINDING STRENGTH IN COVENANT
1 SAMUEL 23:14–18[9]

David escaped to the wilderness of Ziph, while Saul continued to pursue his life daily. This wilderness of Ziph means "melting place." His sojourn reminds us of the believers under intense persecution in the Book of Hebrews who wandered from place to place and obtained a good report.[10] Is there any benefit to persecution or trouble? When tested, the ultimate plan of God is that we come out as gold and obtain a good report. When people come under intense persecution, their values and beliefs are challenged. They could stay true to them, or compromise and change them in order to get out of the furnace. Resentment toward God and those opposing the believer is also possible. In order to have a good report, the test must bring the best, not the worst, out of us.

David, like the saints who were under intense persecution, had a heavenly focus, and his attention was on the Lord. His sustenance came from the Lord, as evidenced in the psalm David wrote when Saul pursued him in the wilderness of Ziph. Leaning on the Lord with our whole being should be a way of life, not a way out of crisis.

> Save me, O God, by thy name, and judge me by thy strength. Hear my prayer, O God; give ear to the words of my mouth. For strangers are risen up against me, and oppressors seek after my soul: they have not set God before them. Selah. Behold, God is mine helper: the Lord is with them that uphold my soul. He shall reward evil unto mine enemies: cut them off in thy truth. I will freely sacrifice unto thee: I will praise thy name, O LORD; for it is good. For he hath delivered me out of all trouble: and mine eye hath seen his desire upon mine enemies.
>
> —PSALM 54:1–7

Jonathan came to strengthen David in the wilderness of Ziph. They strengthened their covenant bond. The Word says there is a friend that sticks closer than a brother. Jonathan is a good example. Although he had no familial ties to David, he demonstrated how covenant brothers in the church ought to relate, placing spiritual covenants above natural ties. Although Jonathan went back home, his heart was with his covenant brother David in the wilderness. Covenant relationship will find you anywhere. The visit of Jonathan was important for David because he received strength for his next challenge. Saul was lurking.

God Troubles Your Tormentor: Wilderness of Moan
1 Samuel 23:24–29[11]

As soon as Jonathan departed, the plot thickened, as the Ziphites connived to hand David over to Saul. He escaped to Moan with Saul in close pursuit. God sent diversion because news of a Philistine invasion caused Saul to withdraw his chase; the Lord had stirred up the Philistines. David held his peace, and God diverted the attention of Saul. This was the first time during David's life as a fugitive that he was not running from his enemy, but due to divine intervention, his enemy was fleeing from him.

God is able to recompense trouble to those who trouble His anointed. We must learn that God has many ways to solve a problem. There are no formulas for deliverance from the enemy, but there are principles that, if we follow them, bring God on the scene in His own way and allow Him to work. God has many ways to deliver the righteous from trouble. Here was Saul very close to catching his prey, but God sent trouble his way. God is always ahead of the enemy. Sometimes we worry about how God will deliver us. What is important is that He promises to deliver. David could not have orchestrated the method of his own deliverance. This is like being in the operating room for open heart surgery but staying awake to see how the doctor performs the surgery. You wouldn't be alive to tell the story. How God meets our needs is immaterial. You can be confident that He will do it, honestly.

MAINTAINING A TENDER HEART: ENGEDI
1 SAMUEL 24:12–14[12]

Upon hearing that David was in the wilderness of Engedi, King Saul sent three thousand men after him. Here David cut the robe of Saul, and his heart smote him. David demonstrated that he was not willing to become king by taking the life of the Saul.

David's servants were ready to finish off Saul, he had to convince them not to do so. David called out to the king and proved that he could have eliminated him, yet chose not to. The king was shamed, and retreated only to resume his chase of David another day. For some other person, cutting the king's robe may have meant little, but David had the highest respect for the office of the king and the anointing that God had placed on it. He treated Saul with the respect that was due as king.

Brokenness is demonstrated when a person decides to wait on God instead of taking the law into his or her own hands. David could have reasoned that this was God's way of ending his struggle, as he was tired of living as a fugitive. His soldiers would have supported him, but his heart smote him for cutting the robe of the king. A wild man would have had no problem taking Saul's life and giving a victory testimony. But God was at work in David's heart, and David was able to differentiate the anointing and office of Saul from the character of Saul. Brokenness is putting the flesh under, taking the longer—but godlier—route to achieving our objectives.

Every believer must be treated with respect and honor, because each believer is the temple of God. The ministers of God must be honored because of the anointing and office they occupy. If a minister is in a backslidden state or in doctrinal error, the answer is to pray for him and move on. Some things can weaken a believer's conscience. The heart will harden when there are unconfessed sins, and sin always takes you farther than you want to go. After a while, people start to do things that their hearts would never have allowed them to do previously.

The Bible also teaches that we reap what we sow. David avoided planting seeds that could trouble him later. Many who have been very critical of leadership are unable to bear criticism when they come into leadership themselves. A church must not become a political minefield where believers walk in fear of one another; where different camps plot to unseat one another; where strife, hypocrisy, ethnic division, and blackmail are tools employed to climb the ladder.

PROPHETIC SIGNPOST: DEATH OF SAMUEL
1 SAMUEL 25:1[13]

The death of Samuel must have been very devastating for David. He must have recalled his first encounter with the prophet, the encounter that in many ways led him to his present predicament.

David had been summoned from his duty post where he tended his father's flock. When he arrived home, he found all of his big brothers waiting. Seated with them was the prophet he had heard so much about. Oil was poured on him, and something unusual came upon him that day; from that time on, he was different. When he heard the ranting of Goliath, that special something he had no way of explaining made him feel he could take down the giant. That victory made him famous in Israel, but in the eyes of the king he became a villain.

This reminds me of the passing of the man who confirmed my calling and released me into the ministry. A missionary sent me to see Pastor S. G. Elton for counsel following the crisis that erupted after I received the Holy Spirit baptism. I had become active outside my denomination and desired to go into the ministry. When I met the prophet, he simply said, "There is no doubt that you are called into the ministry, and the Lord wants you to go on your own." He went on to prophesy some of the things my family and I are doing today.

I was not looking forward to starting my own ministry. In fact, I requested he send me to some other senior minister. About a year later, he died. I remember receiving the news of his death and falling across the bed crying, wondering what would happen to me. Who would mentor me? I had thought if things did not work out well I could return to him and ask how I should proceed. There are paths in life that you have to walk alone. People may speak into your life, but there comes a time you must walk your own walk and dig your own wells. It does not matter how great the mentors are; you must carry your own cross. A mentor can show you the way, but you must walk the road yourself.

The departure of Samuel was prophetic. He had anointed David but was not alive to see him become king. It was, however, a signpost, because the Word of the Lord will never fall to the ground. The pursuit of David by Saul had become fiercer toward the end of Samuel's life. It was a signal in the spirit that the end was near for Saul. The host of darkness would rather destroy God's choice, but the word had been spoken.

The departure of godly men who prophesy revival is always a sign that the time of fulfillment of that purpose is closer. In recent years we have witnessed the home-going of some of the stalwarts of the faith. Some prophesied a great move of God and were sent by God as pioneers of the move. It is an indication that the set time for those prophecies is closer, and we must begin to intercede and birth and bring forth these things in the Spirit.

We must also remember the end of an era is not the end of destiny. David must have been shaken by the passing of a father figure, one whose prophetic words released him into his destiny and started the greatest challenge of his life. When my earthly father went home to be with the Lord, there was a definite sense of loss, especially as it was within a month of the passing of a spiritual mentor, a missionary woman whom God sent to be a spiritual mother to me. The Lord reminded me that the passing of these mentors were signposts on my journey. They fulfilled their roles and ministry to us on the earth, and we are getting closer and deeper into the purposes of God. The batons have been passed to us to finish the race set before us.

The Bible records the passing of Samuel the prophet in one verse. This was Samuel, who was mighty in stature, a national prophet, a man who anointed kings, a prophet whose presence anywhere in Israel brought reverence, a man who succeeded Eli, the man who had prophesied his birth. He was gone, and the Bible records this in one verse. This is a reminder that no one is indispensable. When you put your hand in a bucket of water, you occupy space; when the hand is removed, the space disappears. "You can only work while it is day," Jesus said.[14] When the work is done, you must proceed to your reward.

Jesus alone remains the King who will be worshiped throughout eternity. The greatest of men will only have an epitaph on their grave. It is the lives that we touch that count. They are here today and gone tomorrow, and others must take their place.

TAMING RIGHTEOUS INDIGNATION
1 SAMUEL 25:23–31[15]

David's men had protected the flock of Nabal. Despite their lack of basic necessities, they had not taken advantage of them. Nabal had prospered and was shearing his sheep. David felt this was the right time for Nabal to show his appreciation for their selfless service by sending whatever he had decided as gifts to them. David instructed his men on the right approach. They approached him humbly, with a lot of respect, but he chose to indict David as an ungrateful servant who tried to take the kingdom from King Saul. His servants left with nothing.

David felt shamed and angry. With righteous indignation he decided he was going to wipe out the family of Nabal, but Abigail, Nabal's wife, hearing of her husband's foolish conduct, moved quickly to intercede on behalf of her family. She met David and showed him respect, and apologized for her husband's action. She told David that things would have been different if she had seen his men. She made amends by bringing gifts to David. Abigail identified herself with David's course and pleaded with him to allow God to avenge for him. David was obviously moved by her wisdom. She was a bucket of water to the fire of anger raging in him. She had a calming effect, and her charm and beauty did not go unnoticed; in fact, after Nabal died of a heart attack, David asked Abigail to marry him.

This account clearly demonstrates another area of brokenness. Why was David so quick in his decision to eliminate Nabal but unwilling to kill Saul? Nabal carried no anointing like Saul, but both men had wronged him. Saul had an army and the kingdom with him. Nabal was an ordinary, foolish civilian. Perhaps David felt he could take care of this with no serious consequence or risk. Through the wisdom and counsel of Abigail, he learned to sheath his sword and to allow God to fight for him. For the believer in Christ, the Word clearly teaches that the anger of man is never more effective than the righteousness of God. There are no actions without consequences. When we take revenge for ourselves, we distance ourselves from divine intervention. It takes humility of heart and brokenness to leave judgment with God, especially when you feel you are able to handle the matter without risk or serious consequence to yourself. It is a manifestation of the meekness in Christ. Jesus could have called fire down from heaven, but when He was reviled, He reviled not but committed Himself to God, who judged righteously.

Small actions become turning points because they indicate what we have on the inside. Jesus had the power to release an angelic host against those who treated Him badly. They blasphemed, flogged Him, stripped Him naked, and spat on Him, but He rested in the knowledge that only God could justify Him. He was not interested in becoming a superstar; otherwise his *curriculum vitae* as a servant would have been destroyed. He only wanted to please the Father. He was concerned about service, not office; about fulfilling purpose, not fame. He was broken, like the colt He rode into Jerusalem. All that mattered was to please the one He served: His Father.

GOD PROVES THE HEART
1 SAMUEL 26:8–12[16]

The Ziphites had informed Saul of the location of David in the wilderness of Ziph. Saul mobilized for the chase. He had been in the same wilderness when the Philistines attacked Israel, and he had to give up his chase. This seemed like another opportunity to catch his prey. With the cooperation of the Ziphites he was more confident that he would be victorious, but God had other ideas.

This would be the second time that God would test David by delivering Saul into his hands. Saul had spent the night with his men. Abner, his captain, and others were all soundly asleep in the open camp with Saul's spear and water bottle by his side. David found them just as his spies had reported. Abishai, who accompanied David, was willing to strike the king once, quickly, making sure the king did not suffer much in death, but David wouldn't hear of it. He maintained his earlier position that no one would touch the Lord's anointed.

David called out to Abner with proof that he had not been a good captain. The king's spear and water bottle were in David's hand. Saul realized that David had spared his life twice. He condemned himself before his men and did not seek David again. This may not have been a sign of repentance, as he had made a contrite statement when David spared his life the first time. Saul may have stopped his chase because of David's escape to the land of the Philistines.

Why was this test repeated twice in the life of David? God proves our heart before He promotes us.[17] God was asking David questions. He wanted David to see his own heart. This was a leadership test. Man-made victories are secured by the arm of the flesh, but godly victories require that man does not play God. Places of affliction or trouble are the places where we are graded. These attributes of David were some of the reasons God called him a man after His own heart. If you do not allow the Lord to fight your battles for promotion, you will need to continually fight to keep your seat. David had been inching ever closer to the throne, but the heat of adversity and the threat of attack from King Saul was unrelenting. It seemed the closer he got, the hotter the flames became. He knew if he ever made it to the throne, it would be an act of God, not man.

The notion that it does not matter how you achieve your objective once you dedicate your victory to the Lord is faulty. David could have made it to the throne much earlier, but he refused to transgress spiritual laws. When something is of God, it should have the aroma of heaven. The fruit of the Spirit should be written all over it. A breakthrough that is celebrated but bears corrupt fruit is an abomination before God. Jesus does not believe in victories that are hollow. He told the Pharisees that outward appearances do not fool Him. He is interested in what is on the inside.

God wanted a king who was genuine on the inside; he wanted a king who feared God. After David's second encounter with Saul, the question was, Would David, in desperation, resort to all methods to succeed?

DIVINE INTERVENTION AND PRESERVATION: DAVID SEEKS ASYLUM
1 SAMUEL 27–30

And David said in his heart, I shall now perish one day by the hand of Saul: there is nothing better for me than that I should speedily escape into the land of the Philistines; and Saul shall despair of me, to seek me any more in any coast of Israel: so shall I escape out of his hand. And David arose, and he passed over with the six hundred men that were with him unto Achish, the son of Maoch, king of Gath. And David dwelt with Achish at Gath, he and his men, every man with his household, even David with his two wives, Ahinoam the Jezreelitess, and Abigail the Carmelitess, Nabal's wife. And it was told Saul that David was fled to Gath: and he sought no more again for him.

—1 SAMUEL 27:1–4

David sought political asylum with Achish, king of Gath, in the land of the Philistines. Six hundred men and their families followed David into exile for sixteen months. The king gave him Ziklag as his abode. David continued his raid of enemy territories, including the Amalekites, whom Saul did not utterly destroy.

However, David lied about his true exploits to Achish, king of Gath. The king was made to believe that David had been raiding the land of Israel. Achish felt more confident that the people of Israel would seek to destroy him. In fact, Achish was so confident that he invited David to team up with him as he attacked Israel. However, his men of war were unsure of David's loyalty and refused to allow him to join them in battle.

Divine providence was involved in the decision of King Achish to refuse to allow David to go to war with them. David had done everything to gain the confidence of King Achish, but his men could not be persuaded to allow him to accompany them to war. When God allows a door to close, He might be taking a puzzle piece out of the jigsaw in order to preserve us. Had David gone to war, it is likely that either his men would have killed Saul, or he would have had to turn against the Philistines, who had granted him asylum.

Meanwhile, King Saul was desperate, as the troops of the Philistines marched against him. When there is no depth, men resort to all methods to succeed, and Saul employed the services of a witch to change his fortune. Although he disguised himself, the witch of Endor recognized him. When a leader returns to his vomit, he walks out of grace and into disgrace. When a leader endorses what he erstwhile deemed to be evil and patronizes sin, then the end is near. Saul's end had been prophesied.

David returned to his base in Ziklag only to find out that it had been burned down, and all their families were taken away in a revenge mission by the men of Ziklag, whom he had previously raided.[18] In the midst of the tragedy and confusion these six hundred mighty men of war wept for their families and spoke of stoning David. David learned that when people face personal tragedy, they often make their leaders the scapegoat. Even the closest and the strongest partners can turn against a leader in times of personal tragedy.

There are challenges and fires you may encounter through which those who have been loyal in times past don't have the capacity to help you. For the very first time in the life of David, his own company turned against him. Men who had been with him in his affliction could not understand his fortune because they had been directly targeted. They had not been targeted by their chief foe, Saul, but by another enemy. They were losing their focus. It was not the Amalekites who made them leave Israel; it was Saul, and they were about to self-destruct and award Saul a cheap victory.

In response, David turned to the Lord for direction. He

showed leadership, and his courage was contagious as they all followed him in the recovery effort. He recovered all, and more than he had lost. He sent gifts to the elders of Israel. He instituted a new order in Israel that allowed the same benefits to accrue for those who go to war and those who keep the baggage. Otherwise, the men who were faint from chasing the Philistines would have been denied equal benefit by his soldiers.

The Lord Jesus had to face Gethsemane alone by the strength of God. The disciples slept while He needed them to pray. Leaders must realize that people who do not carry your call do not have the grace to bear your cross. Walk alone if you have to, but walk with God.

KINGDOM MINDEDNESS: DAVID MOURNS THE LORD'S ANOINTED
2 SAMUEL 1–6

Now it came to pass after the death of Saul, when David was returned from the slaughter of the Amalekites, and David had abode two days in Ziklag; It came even to pass on the third day, that, behold, a man came out of the camp from Saul with his clothes rent, and earth upon his head: and so it was, when he came to David, that he fell to the earth, and did obeisance. And David said unto him, From whence comest thou? And he said unto him, Out of the camp of Israel am I escaped. And David said unto him, How went the matter? I pray thee, tell me. And he answered, That the people are fled from the battle, and many of the people also are fallen and dead; and

Saul and Jonathan his son are dead also. And David said unto the young man that told him, How knowest thou that Saul and Jonathan his son be dead? And the young man that told him said, As I happened by chance upon mount Gilboa, behold, Saul leaned upon his spear; and, lo, the chariots and horsemen followed hard after him. And when he looked behind him, he saw me, and called unto me. And I answered, Here am I. And he said unto me, Who art thou? And I answered him, I am an Amalekite. He said unto me again, Stand, I pray thee, upon me, and slay me: for anguish is come upon me, because my life is yet whole in me. So I stood upon him, and slew him, because I was sure that he could not live after that he was fallen: and I took the crown that was upon his head, and the bracelet that was on his arm, and have brought them hither unto my lord. Then David took hold on his clothes, and rent them; and likewise all the men that were with him: And they mourned, and wept, and fasted until even, for Saul, and for Jonathan his son, and for the people of the LORD, and for the house of Israel; because they were fallen by the sword. And David said unto the young man that told him, Whence art thou? And he answered, I am the son of a stranger, an Amalekite. And David said unto him, How wast thou not afraid to stretch forth thine hand to destroy the LORD's anointed? And David called one of the young men, and said, Go near, and fall upon him. And he smote him that he died. And David said unto him, Thy blood be upon thy head; for thy mouth hath testified against thee, saying, I have slain the LORD's anointed. And David lamented with this lamentation over Saul and over Jonathan his son: (Also he bade them teach the children of Judah the use of the bow: behold, it is written in the book of Jasher.) The beauty of Israel is slain upon thy high places: how are the mighty fallen! Tell it not in Gath, publish it not in the streets of Askelon; lest the daughters of the Philistines rejoice, lest the daughters of the uncircumcised triumph. Ye mountains of Gilboa, let there be no dew, neither let there be rain, upon you, nor fields of offerings: for there the shield of the mighty is vilely cast away, the shield of Saul, as though he had not been anointed with oil. From the blood of the slain, from the fat of the mighty, the bow of Jonathan turned not back, and the sword of Saul returned not empty. Saul and Jonathan were lovely and pleasant in their lives, and in their death they were not divided: they were swifter than eagles, they were stronger than lions. Ye daughters of Israel, weep over Saul, who clothed you in scarlet, with other delights, who put on ornaments of gold upon your apparel. How are the mighty fallen in the midst of the battle! O Jonathan, thou wast slain in thine high places. I am distressed for thee, my brother Jonathan: very pleasant hast thou been unto me: thy love to me was wonderful, passing the love of women. How are the mighty fallen, and the weapons of war perished!

—2 SAMUEL 1:1–27

The Philistines had injured Saul in the war. While the chase was on, he begged his armor bearer to end his life, lest he be captured by the enemies, but the armor bearer refused. Saul then fell on his own sword. Saul and his three sons, including Jonathan, were dead.

The Amalekite who brought the news of their deaths reported that he helped Saul to end his life while he was in the throes of death after falling upon his own sword. He received a rude shock. He had brought the news of Saul's death to David expecting him to be happy and possibly receive a reward for his effort. Instead, David was furious that an uncircumcised man who had no covenant was not afraid to touch the Lord's anointed. This demonstrates the reverence David had for the anointing of the Lord. He stood in awe of the Lord and anyone whom the Lord had anointed or who was identified with the Lord.

David was livid with anger, and the Amalekite was summarily executed. This may seem like an extreme reaction, but it demonstrates to us that those who are anointed for ministry offices must be honored. They are not celebrities, but rather servants. However, the oil or anointing upon them cannot be bought with money. No material value can be placed on it. If we honor the Owner of the anointing, we must not despise those He has anointed. The anointing is holy. This does not exonerate the backslidden life of Saul, but the calling and office he stood in is holy.

In the new covenant, all believers are anointed, because the Holy Spirit dwells within us, which is why the Bible says we are the temple of the Holy Spirit. When the focus is on the flesh and its weaknesses, we may not fully appreciate the new creation in Christ.

David recognized that the failure of leadership was a corporate disgrace. He saw beyond Saul to the kingdom. His sojourn in the wilderness and exile deepened his understanding that though Saul was opposing him for personal reasons, the kingdom was bigger than he was. We are all members of that kingdom; a defeat to one is a defeat to all. In the kingdom there is ranking, but leaders are servants, not lords. The kingdom is bigger than any ministry or church. The failure of leadership is therefore a cooperate disgrace. We are all stones in one building. Imagine if a brick in the wall of your house was removed; there would be a gaping hole that would affect the beauty of your house.

How many times have we seen leaders who feel their church and ministries are bigger than the kingdom of God? In the kingdom of God we only have one King, one Hero, one Superstar, one Master, one Savior. He is Jesus. It is all about Him and not about us.

David mourned Jonathan, who he called his brother, because covenant makes us brothers. Jonathan was riding on the wrong boat. Those who rode with Jonah ended up sinking with him until they threw him out. A good person in the wrong company will receive the recompense of the wicked.

Jesus is the Friend that sticks closer than a brother because the blood covenant in Christ is a divine bond stronger than any natural tie. People must see beyond ethnic, social, and racial boundaries, as we are all one in Christ. After the resurrection of Jesus, we do not read about genealogies. All we read about is that God is the Father of spirits and the new creation.

In order to bring out godly character in the believer, God expects us to exercise ourselves in godliness.[19] We may know what the Word says, but for transformation to come we are required to put into practice what we have read or have been taught in the crises of life. David had mega crises, but they drove him closer to the Lord. He had godly exercise every time a challenge came against him. An immature, egotistic, unbroken person would have thrown a thanksgiving party upon learning of the demise of Saul. But David had been walking through the valleys of death. He had reviewed his situation, checked his motives, prayed, sought the Lord, and asked many questions. He had passed several tests and was ready to be king. A depth had been instilled in David, and he was now ready for the next level.

5

TOTAL SURRENDER

EXPERIENCES OF BROKENNESS
REVEAL WHERE YOU ARE
MARK 14:32–41,[1] HEBREWS 5:7–9[2]

THE LORD JESUS, in the Garden of Gethsemane, had the choice to reject the cross. It was not only the physical death that weighed on His mind. Even more was the spiritual death, to be separated from His heavenly Father. To carry the stench of sin, to become the sin substitute and swallow the curses of humanity is beyond what any human being can comprehend. He was about to take on a nature that was foreign and wicked. He was about to become Satan's captive. If there was a time to reconsider his decision, this was the time.

Gethsemane was a place of surrender and brokenness,

as He said yes to God's will. There was a struggle. His flesh wrestled. He offered deep prayers with tears before the Father, but He decided to yield to God's will. This meant He had to go through suffering and death for others, and through that sacrifice He has given life to humanity. Jesus taught that except the grain of wheat falls to the ground and dies, it is just a grain. (See John 12:24.) Jesus learned obedience through His suffering.

The depth of humility in the Lord Jesus accounted for the glory that was given to Him after the resurrection. God highly exalted Him, but He went down before He was raised up and lifted high. How much God will do through us is dependent on how much we allow God to do in us.

Brokenness is a daily affair. Paul said, "I die daily." Every day we must live a surrendered life. It is a journey in godliness. Because we are not robots but have a free will, we must choose to follow the will of God every day. In some areas we may come into a rest quicker than in other areas. God also gives special encounters in areas where they are needed, like we have studied in some of the Bible characters.

We must also differentiate between a person walking in his gifting and office and a life that is bearing character fruit. The office or gifting is not a hallmark of spiritual maturity. A person may prophesy, heal the sick, see visions, and operate in the gifts well while they are backslidden. God speaking through Balaam's donkey is an eloquent testimony to His policy of using anyone, even the backslidden, for a while. The Corinthian church came behind in no gift, yet they were labeled as carnal. Practices which were frowned upon in the world were condoned in their midst.

Saul came and prophesied, although his real goal was to arrest David and kill him. But God detained him as he prophesied and lay naked so that David could escape. God is a smart investor. He will use you until you are unusable, but that does not translate to brokenness or spiritual maturity. It is the Garden of Gethsemane experiences in your life that reveal where you are. Your personal walk with the Lord precedes your public ministry, just as Jesus was tested in the wilderness before He went into his public ministry.

PREPARATION OF INCENSE:
THE NATURE OF MINISTRY
EXODUS 30:35-36[3]

In the preparation of incense, spices such as stacte, onycha, galbanum, and pure frankincense, were used. They were beaten very small and were to be burnt. The word *incense* in Latin means "to burn." Incense was used in worship and was acceptable to the Lord. The perfume coming out of these spices was distinct and was sacred for worship only. This is symbolic of the nature of ministry; we must be beaten small and set on fire before our services can be acceptable.

What does this process entail? As we have seen in this study, God calls us, and He begins a process of removing the chaff from the outer shell. We must put to death things of the flesh. The grain must die so that the real life of God on the inside may be seen. We must be beaten small like the spices of incense and set on fire so the glory of God can be manifested. As we walk with the Lord daily during this process of transformation we are living sacrifices, as the fire of God consumes all the chaff in our lives and only Jesus is seen and glorified.

Smith Wigglesworth said the Lord told him, "Wigglesworth, I am going to burn you all up, until there is no more Wigglesworth, only Jesus."[4] A living sacrifice is a person who surrenders totally to God and has only one focus: to allow Jesus to be seen in his life. It would appear sometimes like he is literally set on fire when he must choose the will of God instead of what is convenient, when he needs to take the longer route instead of a shortcut, and when he needs to walk in meekness and swallow his pride. Jesus went through this fire in Gethsemane. He went through it when He was mocked and reduced to a laughingstock, an object of derision. But His goal was to please the Father.

Fruitfulness and Christlikeness follows this pattern, and there is no fruitfulness without death; there is no incense without brokenness and fire. You may offer your spices of incense unbroken and unbeaten. You may offer time without fire, but they are unacceptable before the Father.

The Lord Jesus Himself was a branch plugged out of fire. Zechariah 3:1–4 is prophetic about the Lord Jesus, as the name Jesus in Hebrew, *Jehoshuah* or *Joshua*, signifies "Savior," or "Jehovah saves."

> And he shewed me Joshua the high priest standing
> before the angel of the Lord, and Satan standing
> at his right hand to resist him. And the LORD said

unto Satan, The LORD rebuke thee, O Satan; even the LORD that hath chosen Jerusalem rebuke thee: is not this a brand plucked out of the fire? Now Joshua was clothed with filthy garments, and stood before the angel. And he answered and spake unto those that stood before him, saying, Take away the filthy garments from him. And unto him he said, Behold, I have caused thine iniquity to pass from thee, and I will clothe thee with change of raiment.

The devil was rebuked because this brand had been plucked out of fire. Jesus had paid His dues. He had fulfilled the mandate of the Father, bearing the stench of spiritual abuse and enduring the worst indignity imaginable, dying the death of the cross. Consequently, the father was pleased with His sacrifice. The aroma of incense came from a life that was well beaten and put on fire. This is the pattern of ministry.

Jesus fully paid the price, and there can be no negotiation with the devil about what belongs to the believer. When a product has been properly produced, its impact on the lives of others is a testimony. It pleased the Lord to bruise the Lord Jesus when Jesus offered Himself as a sacrifice of a sweet smelling savor, just like the spices of incense were beaten small.[5]

BROKENNESS: THE DREDGING OF RIVERS

Dredging allows the river to be cleansed of toxins and accumulated junk that have settled into the river after many years. Some have come as a result of rain washing things from the shore into the river. The depth of the river is also affected because of accumulation of debris and rubbish. A deep river would be able to allow heavier vessels to come through. The depth of the river determines how safe heavy vessels coming through will be. God may not allow certain heavy-duty operations in the church if the river is not deepened and cleansed.

It is true that we become new creations in Christ when we get saved and may even surrender to the Lord. Our surrender to the Lord will be tested along the way. Satan will challenge the decision. On our own we may allow things to slip or allow sin to clutter the river. What causes shallowness in the river is the dumping of waste in the river. After a while the river becomes sluggish. A river that is full of debris has to be dredged in order for big vessels to ply the route. In the church, we need to allow the big vessels of the Holy Spirit to pass through our spiritual waters, but if we are shallow He cannot come through or manifest at the level at which He desires to manifest.

No wonder Paul says all things are lawful but not all things are expedient. There are attitudes, habits, and mindsets in the church that clutter the rivers of God. It then becomes dangerous for the Holy Spirit to bring the bigger vessels of the Spirit through. Imagine Ananias and Sapphira, who did not disclose the exact amount of their land transaction, although they still gave to the church. They met their death. Consider the number of believers who made pledges and don't even remember the pledges today.

The water was deeper, and the big vessels were in it. God in His mercy has held some glory back to keep death and destruction from the church, but the time has now come in

God's timetable for the glory to be revealed. We must shape up or be shipped out.

Brokenness or inner dredging gives us the capacity to carry more, convey more of the glory of God. A shallow river is dangerous to the vessel. God will use our challenges and tests to help us minister to others. When the river is shallow, we manifest power like the world, wealth like the world, and fame like the world; and of course, they see no difference. It has little impact. Just plenty of smoke, but no fire. A sheep that gets into the mud is quick to get out, but when the flesh outweighs the spirit, believers can be found wanting. The real sacrifice is to keep God's habitation free of clutter. To be quick to repent is to be contrite. The heart that is yielded to the Lord will live with the pulse of heaven.

David wanted to clean out the sin and clutter in his life. He was not interested in officialdom or title, unlike Saul, who wanted to maintain the image rather than the relationship. David knew God sees beyond the façade and will not manifest Himself in an unbroken vessel. David had committed terrible sins, adultery and murder. He tried to cover up his wrongdoing, but God exposed David, and he could not run; the ghosts of his past had caught up with him. David's spiritual riverbed was filled with debris and rubbish. The office he occupied, his prophetic gifts, his past achievements notwithstanding, he was deep in mud and mire. His river needed dredging; he needed brokenness.

David had to expose his heart to God's searchlight. His spirit was sorrowful, repentant, broken, which is the real sacrifice God wants. It means keeping the heart tender, making sure there are no sins, attitudes, or faults that can clutter the river of God within us.

In Psalm 51:10–17[6] David prays for a clean heart. He cries out to God for His abiding presence. He confesses his sins of murder, lies, and conspiracy. This was not a time for cover-up or maintaining appearances. He was desperate for the presence of God and divine intimacy. He purged himself.

George Stormont gives the following account of time he spent with Smith Wigglesworth and what he learned about the keys to Wigglesworth's power:

> When Smith Wigglesworth stayed in our home once, he came down early one morning and told me, "God spoke to me on your bed." "What did He say?" I asked. He said, "Wigglesworth, I am going to burn you all up, until there is no more Wigglesworth, only Jesus." Standing at the foot of our stairs, he raised his hand to heaven, and with tears running down his cheeks, he cried, "O, God, come and do it! I don't want them to see me anymore—only Jesus!" This was his message; this was his cry. This was the prophetic work that God did in him, and that He must do in all of us, so that we all may be living letters to a dying world. This was the secret of Wigglesworth's power. This is the essence of revival.[7]

There are two extremes in dealing with sin. People can become so sin-conscious that they hunt for sins and demons in their lives or behind every tree. This negates the gift of righteousness that has been given to believers. A believer has

God's nature and does not enjoy sin. On the other hand, the flesh is not saved, and believers who yield to the flesh will have their river cluttered.

David, like Jonah, was in deep trouble and felt unbearable pressure. He began to cry out of the depth of his misery to God. In crisis situations when all hope is gone, people tend to purify their motives. Out of the depth of despair they cry out to God sincerely. The challenges that David faced were of the proportion that cause people to wonder where their God is. At such times soul-searching becomes imperative. We question where we might have missed it. People in this situation, like Jonah, repent and make fresh consecration from the depths of their heart. They reach out to Him. There is no time for a superficial relationship here. This must carry on after the crisis. Jonah repented and the fish vomited him.

In Psalm 42:7 we read that "deep calleth unto deep."[8] The depth of the river will be shown by the purity of the water and depth of the encounter. Water from a deep borehole is clean and safe to drink. You cannot afford to drink from shallow water because of the debris. When ministry comes out of the depths of God on the inside, it is always fresh. There may be no fanfare, but the impact is always eternal and divine. Shallow rivers are noisy, but deep rivers are quiet; you only realize how deep they are when you step in.

The Lord Jesus was not into self-advertisement. He healed people and told them to tell no man. People sought Him everywhere because His words carried power. Encounters with Him meant transformation. So committed was He that He spent time with the Father before setting out. And after

His ministry time He was consistently before the Father. No wonder His words were life changing. His touch brought healing. Miracles were commonplace in His ministry.

As a young man David had experienced genuine fellowship and encounters with the Lord. As a shepherd boy, the presence of God was upon him. As he wrestled wild animals, as he played his harp, he entered into a depth of intimacy. His confidence in his covenant relationship with God was so strong that he challenged a giant and slew him. As he ran away from Saul, he learned to lean on God. He had a taste for God's presence and desired God more than he desired the throne. When he sinned against God, he knew he had lost what was most valuable. He needed a new depth, and from the depth of his despair he cried to God.

Children who are raised in the Lord, who have real encounters with the Lord, and later draw back return to the Lord because they are haunted by the genuine encounter they had before. Once you have genuinely encountered the Lord and you set your affection on Him, all things pale into insignificance.

Lester Sumrall reports that spending time in the presence of Smith Wigglesworth impacted him. Just being in the presence of the man made him different. It was reported of Wigglesworth that strangers often said he convicted them of sin. He lived a life where his purpose was that people should see Jesus, not him. The mere presence of some people can have an impact in silence, while an hour-long sermon from others leaves people dry. Sumrall's report of an encounter between him and Wigglesworth speaks volumes about Wigglesworth's intimacy and depth in God:

> Your body can become weary after hours of this, but it seems to bring a tremendous refreshing to Wigglesworth. Finally, he got up from his knees and began to tell beautiful stories of how God had healed this disease and that condition. I sat there weeping, absolutely overwhelmed. Before I had gone a block from his house, I said to myself, "You know, I got something there. I'm different. I got something. I received a blessing. I received an anointing. Something good happened to me in that place. I'll come back again." I received life in that house. Both father and daughter had life. About ten days later, I went back. Oh, yes, I had on my little dark-blue raincoat, and I had my umbrella and my bowler hat—but I did not have a newspaper! He had made a tremendous amount of money in his overseas meetings, particularly on the continent. But he lived very thriftily, because he funneled the majority of his offering into missions as fast as he got it. He particularly supported Salter's efforts in the Congo. He never cared about the money for himself. He lived *by faith*.[9]

6

BROKENNESS AND HARVEST

I N 1 SAMUEL 1:12[1] we read that Hannah was barren for years. She was brokenhearted as a result of her unacceptable condition, and the relentless taunting from her husband's second wife, Peninnah. She cried to her husband, Elkanah, for help, but this situation was beyond him. He asked her to accept his love as compensation for her childlessness. The continuous harassment from Peninnah made the annual trip to Shiloh to sacrifice to the Lord a traumatic encounter. Often she wept and would not eat. On one of those trips she was troubled, and in bitterness of soul and she began to pray. Her lips were moving, but her words were not audible. She prayed earnestly within her heart. When Eli the prophet noticed this, he assumed she had been drinking.

He rebuked her sternly, but Hannah explained to the prophet that she was not drunk but only heavy in spirit.

Many people lose their harvest when they become easily offended. The defense of her reputation would have stood in the way of her miracle, but dead people have no reputation to defend. The grain that falls to the ground and dies will produce more. Part of dying daily is refusing to allow our flesh to gain the ascendancy in difficult situations. The outer part, or the flesh, of man—which is not saved—is the one that must be put under. It needs to die daily, because the inner man, the re-created human spirit, is a replica of Jesus and has the Holy Spirit within. But the flesh is carnal, earthly, and if allowed, it would act like the devil.

The situation Hannah found herself in was a perfect opportunity for this to happen. She was a woman who had good reason to be angry. She had prayed many years for the same thing. She was not fulfilled in her marriage. Her husband did not understand the stress her childlessness was putting on her. The other wife made her life miserable in private and in public, and now her pastor was calling her a drunken woman while she was in prayer. The pastor forgot to ask her questions before drawing a conclusion. He forgot to use gentle words, but instead was brash, tactless, and crude. In today's world she might have left the church or worked to get on the elder's board to vote out the pastor. Or, she could have started telling her story to others. But she made a different choice: she put her flesh under.

Most times people think of "me." Really, it is the flesh that is being considered. The re-created human spirit is designed to look to God for sustenance. The Word of God and fellowship with the Father are the nourishment of the spirit, but the flesh feeds on earthly and carnal stuff. The flesh must then be put under and allowed to die, in order for the true life in the spirit to emerge.

Hannah did this. She honored a man who dishonored her. She refused to be offended and reaped a harvest of miracles. Not only was Samuel borne, but she had other children as well.

We must also be mindful of our flesh and its tendencies when fellow ministers fall into sin. Our spirit, not our flesh, must be in control. The Word warns us to be careful how we treat fallen ministers, lest our pride take over and we plant a seed that destroys us. Corrections must be made with kindness and grace. Hannah honored a man whose home was not in order, a man God rebuked for honoring his children above Him, a man to whom God said his sin would never be wiped out—and she got a miracle. We are not supposed to follow their wicked or pernicious ways, but we must honor the grace and leave the judgment to God. It is a heart matter.

Luke 4:14–30[2] tells us of a time when Jesus was in His hometown and could there do no mighty works, because their flesh rose up to question His credibility. They had known Him as a carpenter; He had probably had made some furniture for them while working under His earthly father, Joseph.

I cannot help but think about the brokenness Jesus Himself demonstrated when He agreed to come to this world He had created. He was born a baby, stripping Himself of all powers, and then was rejected by those He came to serve. Yet

He was not bitter. Their fleshly competition and naive arrogance rose up to challenge His credentials. They questioned Him and probably reminded Him of the controversial nature of His birth. They were convinced that He was not the Son of God, as His earthly brothers and sisters were still living among them. For all they cared, this man was an impostor who should be paid no attention. This was their flesh. We cannot choose the agent of our deliverance; we must not allow offense to rob us of divine visitation.

Believers can be trapped in the same attitude in which the flesh refuses to accept the call and grace on others because of their natural credentials. It is common knowledge that close family members struggle to receive ministry from one another, and this is part of the reason why. The flesh needs to die to work in greater harvest.

The same Jesus went elsewhere and was honored, and performed great miracles. Jesus was not living by the dictates of the flesh. He did not try to prove any point; He simply ministered to those who were willing to be prayed for. Although His kinsmen challenged him to replicate the same miracles He had done in other places to prove to them He was anointed, Jesus was in no contest with anyone and did not need their approval to validate His ministry. He was dead to censure or praise.

A modern-day minister might have acted differently. He might have used good advertisements and videos of past miracles to prove a point or get a professional marketing firm to craft the introduction and arrange endorsements with the important clergy in the area. Jesus simply ministered to those in need and moved on. The measure of a man's ministry is not in the endorsements from others, but in the affirmation of the Father. Jesus's flesh was dead to the drumbeat of earthly praise. Jesus answered the question of how to respond when people do not receive your ministry:

- He did not change His calling, but He affirmed it.
- He helped those who were willing to be helped.
- He recognized that you cannot minister to those who refuse to receive you.
- He refused to get into a fight.
- He left and refused to allow them to kill Him.
- He demonstrated that those to whom you are sent will receive you. Your harvest and impact will abound where there is acceptance and expectation.

Jesus gave the example of the widow of Zarephath, who took care of the prophet Elijah. She was a foreigner. She lived in the area of jurisdiction of that city that was inhabited by Gentiles. God providing for His prophet first by an unclean bird and then by a Gentile whom the Jews esteemed unclean, was a clear demonstration that God looks for willing hearts anywhere. In the account of Elijah and this Gentile widow, the Word says that God had commanded her to feed the prophet. How did He do this? We do not have a record of how, but it is clear that she was a woman who was open to the Lord, able to hear God in the austere times when resources were limited and *survival* was the keyword. I believe the Lord prepared her heart. He saw that she was willing on the inside. Jesus was saying God sees the heart and would not waste His grace where people are not willing to receive what He has to offer.

This explains why two people can attend the same service, and one is mightily blessed, while the other is not. Jesus made it clear that the problem was not with the supply of grace but the reception of it. When the flesh is in ascendancy, people focus on the outside rather than the inside, but God looks on the inside.

Jesus also gave the example of Naaman, to whom Elisha was sent. His willingness was not immediate. He struggled with his flesh. He was a commander with great accomplishments, greatly loved by his king, but he was a leper. He was fully prepared to pay his medical bill, and he brought plenty other valuables to show his appreciation. He received a rather rude reception. He expected the prophet to show up and give him a dignified welcome as a man of great standing in society, but the prophet only sent one of his servants with an instruction.

The instruction was shocking to Naaman, who was already questioning the breach of diplomatic protocol from the prophet and the nation. He was to dip seven times in the Jordan River to be healed. This only compounded his frustration and sense of indignation. He flew off the handle and was visibly angry. He was ready to head home but for the wise and timely intervention of his servants, who encouraged him to obey the simple instruction. He went to the Jordan, put his flesh under, and was healed. This whole process was no doubt humiliating. He knew of better rivers where he could have bathed at home.

Jesus said Elisha was sent to Naaman. This means people to whom we are sent may need to overcome certain human hindrances before they can receive. It is important, however, to note that Elisha never changed his position. He did not respond to the temper tantrums of Naaman. He sat quietly until Naaman made the adjustments and received. The message remains the same for ministry. Our methods may change to reach different generations, but we are not called to violate ministerial ethics in order to include everyone. Neither are we to indulge and massage people's egos in order to carry them along.

Naaman made a change on the inside, but the people in Jesus's hometown were not interested in changing on the inside. Their minds were set. Their egos and sensibilities had been insulted by a man whose patrimony was a subject of debate, a man who had worked as a carpenter, whose siblings were well known to them. They could not accept that God would use their hometown boy and not them. Someone far away with better credentials would have been in a better position to minister to them, so they thought. But God plays by a different set of rules. We cannot receive from those we fail to honor. In the account of Luke, after Jesus had spoken from the Book of Isaiah, confirming the prophecy that He was the Anointed One, they rose to kill Him. This is a demonic pattern. They had an idea who the Messiah would be, but definitely not Mary and Joseph's son, not a hometown boy. You can do nothing about those who reject you, so Jesus left. He loved them, but He left them.

There are situations in which God does not want you to live. Had Jesus remained, His ministry would have been hampered. The people in His hometown had become the jury, and their verdict was in. There is a time to dust your feet and leave.

Jesus carried the cross, a symbol of shame, for no wrong that He had done—and for those people who rejected Him. Everyone who follows the Lord must take up his own cross daily. This is putting the flesh to death daily.

The Old Testament sin offering had to be led outside the camp and sent away. Jesus carried His cross in shame outside the gate, or without the camp. The writer of Hebrews says we must be prepared to suffer shame for what we believe, even if it means being excluded like that sacrificial lamb.[3] I have lived in a nation where people have paid the supreme price for their faith, and lost their lives. Paul and the early apostles paid dearly for what we now have. We must be prepared to put the flesh down, to allow the power of God in the new creation to rise within us to live victoriously over sin. Our lives should be different than those of the world by daily trusting in the power of His grace to put down the flesh. We can be light and salt to our world.

We must ask ourselves, How much are we ready to suffer for what we believe? Or, how much are we ready to hide what we believe in order to be accepted or included? It is amazing how far people go just to get that pat on the back, that mention in the media, or the spotlight in their area. The service or life in God does not thrive on earthly cheers. Peter and the disciples had a hard time understanding why Jesus would not use His rising fame to overthrow the Romans, their tormentors, but instead spoke of giving His life on the cross. Jesus was not concerned about the approval of men. He was calm and firm when those closest to Him disagreed with His mission.

The disciples were dreaming of an earthly government. The mother of the sons of Zebedee already put in a word for her boys, assuming Jesus would establish something on earth. The disciples had also argued about who would be the greatest. So, the idea of Him dying on a cross, the most despicable death meant for criminals, was grotesque and unimaginable. This would end their dreams of prominence, and there would be no answer to the critics who felt they left too much to follow the carpenter from Galilee. Jesus knew their reasoning but was not bothered. Their flesh could not follow the Spirit. They needed to die to their own agendas.

It is strange that the church today is also seeking recognition from the world. Although we are not called to be deliberately obnoxious and unfriendly, to expect the world or carnal Christians to appreciate spiritual commitment only leads to compromise. When we deliberately seek the attention of the world, when the approval of the ungodly becomes our yardstick for spiritual progression, then we are in big trouble. Jesus was never understood by the religious hierarchy of His day. When they attended His seminars, they did not take notes. They looked for ammunition and doctrinal differences to hang Him with. Most of those who followed

Him were not highly rated. Although He had Joseph of Arimathea and other secret disciples, His security was not in the class of men that followed Him but in the approval of His heavenly Father. No wonder He spent a lot of time alone with the Father.

Jesus was completely dead to the need for men's approval or competition. One time the disciples came back with the news that some people were doing miracles in the name of Jesus. He simply told them those people were not competitors but colaborers.

Jesus was also completely committed to the kingdom. He had no problem being baptized by His forerunner, what we call an advance party today, or the ministry of a crusade director, who goes ahead of the man of God. He was secure in His identity, and the flesh had no place to rule in his life.

Herod would have been too glad to improve his profile, had Jesus attempted to meet him. But after John the Baptist was killed, Jesus's message to Herod was that He was not moved by the murder of John. He was committed to His assignment. A more timid minister would have tried to negotiate a truce, change location, retire, or go AWOL. Jesus simply re-fired.

In Matthew 8:5–10[4] we read about the centurion who wanted Jesus to heal his servant but had no preconditions. He belonged to the ruling class, the occupying force. He was in the upper social strata, but he recognized that his position in the flesh could not be used as a spiritual bargaining tool. The flesh naturally would like to show off. How can a man of such position be begging a preacher or minister to come to him? Instead of sending an order to Jesus, he pleaded with Him.

Some believers fail to recognize that their natural accomplishments and position in the world are no passport to spiritual ascendancy and should give them no edge over others. Ministries are sometimes guilty of using natural status as the yardstick for spiritual promotion. Many times, people without calling are lifted to ministry positions so their natural advantage can be utilized by the church. But the centurion's humility and ability to put his flesh down gave him a healing harvest, to which Jesus commented that He had not found so great a faith in Israel.

Many times our attitude can deny the expression of our faith. God wants to bless us, but He also wants to see the fruit of godliness in our lives. Take the example of the Canaanite woman who needed deliverance for her demon-possessed young daughter.[5] She had every reason to be angry at Jesus. She would have had many supporters in the church today who would have called Jesus prejudiced and racist. Of course, He was none of these; He wanted to see her faith and her character.

She had followed, worshiping. Her persistence was driving the disciples up the wall. They felt pressured, disturbed, and were tired of her nagging request. Her daughter was sick, but since Jesus was not really paying attention to her, they felt she ought to have relented. Jesus told the woman that He needed to focus on the Jews before Gentiles. He even used the derogatory term used for people of that region, which was *dog* to address her. Many would have questioned His spirituality and sensitivity at this point. However, Jesus was testing her heart just to see how determined she was and if offense would stand in her way. When the flesh is not dead we are easily offended; we wear our feelings on our sleeves. This woman had a bigger purpose than her flesh: her daughter needed a miracle.

Sometimes the uncrucified flesh becomes a roadblock to healing, but this woman worshiped Jesus and told Him she was not there to argue about how people perceived her or what the cultural taboos were. She honored and recognized Jesus as a kind Master who would allow little crumbs to fall from the table to the dogs. She was sure that the little crumbs would be more than sufficient to drive out the demons from her daughter. This situation would have set many back wondering about the love of God and questioning the integrity of Jesus. The flesh wants to be noticed, praised, and fulfilled. This woman looked past that, and went home to find her prayer answered, and her daughter healed.

We are enjoined in Scripture to be at peace with all men, especially those of the household of faith. Some of the contention that breaks our churches is simply people's fleshly reaction to the will of God. This woman was not interested in the merit or demerit of the social stigma for which she and her daughter were labeled. She simply focused on what was most important to her, the healing of her child. Believers must focus on what is important and save vital energy for serving the Lord instead of engaging in all the small fights that rob the church of grace. There are things to be confronted, but do not allow bitterness to rob you of blessings in your own life.

Furthermore, there is a fine line between idolizing a

minister and reverencing the anointing a minister carries. The rule of the thumb should be to honor the minister and the anointing but to let Jesus remain our Standard. We must be careful not to dishonor the Lord in an effort to honor the grace given to God's servant; Jesus must remain our Standard. The minister may fail, but Jesus, our Standard and Hero, cannot fail. Even if the minister falls short of the Word of God, we must keep our focus on Jesus.

BIBLIOGRAPHY

Damazio, Frank. *The Making of a Leader.* Portland, OR: Bible Temple Publishing, 1988.

Hagin, E. Kenneth. *Must Christians Suffer?* Tulsa, OK: Faith Library Publications, 1982.

Maddon J. Peter. *The Keys to Wigglesworth's Power.* New Kensington, PA: Whitaker House, 2000.

Renner, Rick. *If You Were God, Would You Choose You?* Tulsa, OK: Rick Renner Ministries, 1999.

Sumrall, Lester. *Pioneers of Faith.* South Bend, IN: Harrison House, 1995.

Wigglesworth, Smith. *The Complete Collection of His Life Teachings.* Compiled by Roberts Liardon. Tulsa, OK: Albury Publishing, 1996.

NOTES

CHAPTER 1

1. "And Jesus answered them, saying, The hour is come, that the Son of man should be glorified. Verily, verily, I say unto you, Except a corn of wheat fall into the ground and die, it abideth alone: but if it die, it bringeth forth much fruit" (John 12:23).

2. "I protest by your rejoicing which I have in Christ Jesus our Lord, I die daily" (1 Cor. 15:31).

3. "Behold we put bits in the horses' mouths, that they may obey us; and we turn about their whole body" (James 3:3).

4. "And I, brethren, could not speak unto you as unto spiritual, but as unto carnal, even as unto babes in Christ" (1 Cor. 3:1). "Because the carnal mind is enmity against God: for it is not subject to the law of God, neither indeed can be" (Rom. 8:7).

5. "Neither do men light a candle, and put it under a bushel, but on a candlestick; and it giveth light unto all that are in the house" (Matt. 5:15).

6. "But made himself of no reputation, and took upon him the form of a servant, and was made in the likeness of men" (Phil. 2:7).

7. "And lo a voice from heaven, saying, This is my beloved Son, in whom I am well pleased" (Matt. 3:17).

8. "Though he were a Son, yet learned he obedience by the things which he suffered" (Heb. 5:8).

9. "Submit yourselves therefore to God. Resist the devil, and he will flee from you" (James 4:7).

10. "It seemed good unto us, being assembled with one accord, to send chosen men unto you with our beloved Barnabas and Paul, men that have hazarded their lives for the name of our Lord Jesus Christ" (Acts 15:25–26).

11. "For the love of money is the root of all evil: which while some coveted after, they have erred from the faith, and pierced themselves through with many sorrows" (1 Tim. 6:10).

12. "And when they came nigh to Jerusalem, unto Bethphage and Bethany, at the mount of Olives, he sendeth forth two of his disciples, And saith unto them, Go your way into the village over against you: and as soon as ye be entered into it, ye shall find a colt tied, whereon never man sat; loose him, and bring him. And if any man say unto you, Why do ye this? say ye that the Lord hath need of him; and straightway he will send him hither. And they went their way, and found the colt tied by the door without in a place where two ways met; and they loose him. And certain of them that stood there said unto them, What do ye, loosing the colt? And they said unto them even as Jesus had commanded: and they let them go. And they brought the colt to Jesus, and cast their garments on him; and he sat upon him. And many spread their garments in the way: and others cut down branches off the trees, and strawed them in the way. And they that went before, and they that followed, cried, saying, Hosanna; Blessed is he that cometh in the name of the Lord: Blessed be the kingdom of our father David, that cometh in the name of the Lord: Hosanna in the highest" (Mark 11:1–10).

13. "Let this mind be in you, which was also in Christ Jesus: Who, being in the form of God, thought it not robbery to be equal with God: But made himself of no reputation, and took upon him the form of a servant, and was made in the likeness of men: And being found in fashion as a man, he humbled himself, and became obedient unto death, even the death of the cross" (Phil. 2:5–8).

14. Peter J. Maddon, *The Keys to Wigglesworth's Power* (New Kensington, PA: Whitaker House) Kathryn Kuhlman, 163–164.

CHAPTER 2

1. "And Jacob was left alone; and there wrestled a man with him until the breaking of the day. And when he saw that he prevailed not against him, he touched the hollow of his thigh; and the hollow of Jacob's thigh was out of joint, as he wrestled with him. And he

said, Let me go, for the day breaketh. And he said, I will not let thee go, except thou bless me. And he said unto him, What is thy name? And he said, Jacob. And he said, Thy name shall be called no more Jacob, but Israel: for as a prince hast thou power with God and with men, and hast prevailed. And Jacob asked him, and said, Tell me, I pray thee, thy name. And he said, Wherefore is it that thou dost ask after my name? And he blessed him there. And Jacob called the name of the place Peniel: for I have seen God face to face, and my life is preserved. And as he passed over Penuel the sun rose upon him, and he halted upon his thigh" (Gen. 32:24–31).

2. "He took his brother by the heel in the womb, and by his strength he had power with God: Yea, he had power over the angel, and prevailed. He wept and made supplication unto him: he found him in Bethel, and there he spake with us" (Hosea 12:3–4).

3. "And as he passed over Penuel the sun rose upon him, and he halted upon his thigh" (Gen. 32:31).

4. "Peter answered and said unto him, Though all men shall be offended because of thee, yet will I never be offended. Jesus said unto him, Verily I say unto thee, That this night, before the cock crow, thou shalt deny me thrice. Peter said unto him, Though I should die with thee, yet will I not deny thee. Likewise also said all the disciples.... Now Peter sat without in the palace: and a damsel came unto him, saying, Thou also wast with Jesus of Galilee. But he denied before them all, saying, I know not what thou sayest. And when he was gone out into the porch, another maid saw him, and said unto them that were there, This fellow was also with Jesus of Nazareth. And again he denied with an oath, I do not know the man. And after a while came unto him they that stood by, and said to Peter, Surely thou also art one of them; for thy speech bewrayeth thee. Then began he to curse and to swear, saying, I know not the man. And immediately the cock crew. And Peter remembered the word of Jesus, which said unto him, Before the cock crow, thou shalt deny me thrice. And he went out, and wept bitterly" (Matt. 26:33–36, 69–75).

5. "And the Lord turned, and looked upon Peter. And Peter remembered the word of the Lord, how he had said unto him, Before the cock crow, thou shalt deny me thrice. And Peter went out, and wept bitterly" (Luke 22:61–62).

6. "And he shall sit as a refiner and purifier of silver: and he shall purify the sons of Levi, and purge them as gold and silver, that they may offer unto the Lord an offering in righteousness. Then shall the

offering of Judah and Jerusalem be pleasant unto the LORD, as in the days of old, and as in former years" (Mal. 3:3–4).

7. "He weakened my strength in the way; he shortened my days" (Ps. 102:23).

8. "And it came to pass, after the year was expired, at the time when kings go forth to battle, that David sent Joab, and his servants with him, and all Israel; and they destroyed the children of Ammon, and besieged Rabbah. But David tarried still at Jerusalem. And it came to pass in an eveningtide, that David arose from off his bed, and walked upon the roof of the king's house: and from the roof he saw a woman washing herself; and the woman was very beautiful to look upon" (2 Sam. 11:1–2).

9. Andrew Murray, *Absolute Surrender*, PC Study Bible, formatted electronic database Copyright © 2003, 2006 Biblesoft, Inc. All rights reserved.

10. "So when they had dined, Jesus saith to Simon Peter, Simon, son of Jonas, lovest thou me more than these? He saith unto him, Yea, Lord; thou knowest that I love thee. He saith unto him, Feed my lambs. He saith to him again the second time, Simon, son of Jonas, lovest thou me? He saith unto him, Yea, Lord; thou knowest that I love thee. He saith unto him, Feed my sheep. He saith unto him the third time, Simon, son of Jonas, lovest thou me? Peter was grieved because he said unto him the third time, Lovest thou me? And he said unto him, Lord, thou knowest all things; thou knowest that I love thee. Jesus saith unto him, Feed my sheep" (John 21:15–17).

11. "Verily, verily, I say unto thee, When thou wast young, thou girdest thyself, and walkedst whither thou wouldest: but when thou shalt be old, thou shalt stretch forth thy hands, and another shall gird thee, and carry thee whither thou wouldest not. This spake he, signifying by what death he should glorify God. And when he had spoken this, he saith unto him, Follow me" (John 21:18–19).

12. "And Saul was consenting unto his death. And at that time there was a great persecution against the church which was at Jerusalem; and they were all scattered abroad throughout the regions of Judaea and Samaria, except the apostles. And devout men carried Stephen to his burial, and made great lamentation over him. As for Saul, he made havock of the church, entering into every house, and haling men and women committed them to prison" (Acts 8:1–3).

13. "Which when the brethren knew, they brought him down to Caesarea, and sent him forth to Tarsus. Then had the churches rest throughout all Judaea and Galilee and Samaria, and were edified;

and walking in the fear of the Lord, and in the comfort of the Holy Ghost, were multiplied" (Acts 9:30–31).

14. *Robertson New Testament Word Pictures* Power Bible CD 2.1 (electronic commentary.

15. "And I thank Christ Jesus our Lord, who hath enabled me, for that he counted me faithful, putting me into the ministry; Who was before a blasphemer, and a persecutor, and injurious: but I obtained mercy, because I did it ignorantly in unbelief" (1 Tim. 1:12–13).

16. "Behold, I have refined thee, but not with silver; I have chosen thee in the furnace of affliction" (Isa. 48:10).

17. "But what things were gain to me, those I counted loss for Christ. Yea doubtless, and I count all things but loss for the excellency of the knowledge of Christ Jesus my Lord: for whom I have suffered the loss of all things, and do count them but dung, that I may win Christ, And be found in him, not having mine own righteousness, which is of the law, but that which is through the faith of Christ, the righteousness which is of God by faith: That I may know him, and the power of his resurrection, and the fellowship of his sufferings, being made conformable unto his death; If by any means I might attain unto the resurrection of the dead. Not as though I had already attained, either were already perfect: but I follow after, if that I may apprehend that for which also I am apprehended of Christ Jesus. Brethren, I count not myself to have apprehended: but this one thing I do, forgetting those things which are behind, and reaching forth unto those things which are before, I press toward the mark for the prize of the high calling of God in Christ Jesus" (Phil. 3:7–14).

18. "And he said unto them, Ye are they which justify yourselves before men; but God knoweth your hearts: for that which is highly esteemed among men is abomination in the sight of God" (Luke 16:15).

19. "But the God of all grace, who hath called us unto his eternal glory by Christ Jesus, after that ye have suffered a while, make you perfect, stablish, strengthen, settle you" (1 Pet. 5:10).20. Kenneth E. Hagin, *Must Christians Suffer?* (Broken Arrow, OK: Faith Library Publications, 1982), 13, 35.

CHAPTER 3

1. Albert Hibbert, *Smith Wigglesworth: The Secret of His Power* (Tulsa, OK: Harrison House, 1982), 99, available at GoogleBooks, http://books.google.com/books?id=Moqz-x9W_EUC&pg=PA99&lpg=PA99&dq=smith+wigglesworth+you+have+to+live+ready&source=

bl&ots=uZN86pCoaO&sig=1-FVOUFW6rTCEO2bUCBooDVRcIw&
hl=en&ei=EzyrTdvOL4jdoQHc4qX5CA&sa=X&oi=book_result&ct=
result&resnum=2&ved=0CBoQ6AEwAQ#v=onepage&q=smith%20
wigglesworth%20you%20have%20to%20live%20ready&f=false,
accessed April 17, 2011.

2. "And David said unto Saul, Thy servant kept his father's sheep, and there came a lion, and a bear, and took a lamb out of the flock: And I went out after him, and smote him, and delivered it out of his mouth: and when he arose against me, I caught him by his beard, and smote him, and slew him. Thy servant slew both the lion and the bear: and this uncircumcised Philistine shall be as one of them, seeing he hath defied the armies of the living God. David said moreover, The Lord that delivered me out of the paw of the lion, and out of the paw of the bear, he will deliver me out of the hand of this Philistine. And Saul said unto David, Go, and the Lord be with thee" (1 Sam. 17:34–37).

3. "But he that is greatest among you shall be your servant" (Matt. 23:11).

4. "Now I say, That the heir, as long as he is a child, differeth nothing from a servant, though he be lord of all; But is under tutors and governors until the time appointed of the father" (Gal. 4:1–2).

5. Several parallels exist between Jesus and Isaac: Isaac was the only begotten son of Abraham; Jesus was the only begotten Son of God. Isaac carried the wood of sacrifice, and Jesus carried the cross. Isaac was bound, and Jesus was bound. "And it came to pass after these things, that God did tempt Abraham, and said unto him, Abraham: and he said, Behold, here I am. And he said, Take now thy son, thine only son Isaac, whom thou lovest, and get thee into the land of Moriah; and offer him there for a burnt offering upon one of the mountains which I will tell thee of. And Abraham rose up early in the morning, and saddled his ass, and took two of his young men with him, and Isaac his son, and clave the wood for the burnt offering, and rose up, and went unto the place of which God had told him...And they came to the place which God had told him of; and Abraham built an altar there, and laid the wood in order, and bound Isaac his son, and laid him on the altar upon the wood. And Abraham stretched forth his hand, and took the knife to slay his son" (Gen. 22:1–3, 9–10).

6. "But seek ye first the kingdom of God, and his righteousness; and all these things shall be added unto you" (Matt. 6:33).

CHAPTER 4

1. "So David fled, and escaped, and came to Samuel to Ramah, and told him all that Saul had done to him. And he and Samuel went and dwelt in Naioth. And it was told Saul, saying, Behold, David is at Naioth in Ramah. And Saul sent messengers to take David: and when they saw the company of the prophets prophesying, and Samuel standing as appointed over them, the Spirit of God was upon the messengers of Saul, and they also prophesied. And when it was told Saul, he sent other messengers, and they prophesied likewise. And Saul sent messengers again the third time, and they prophesied also. Then went he also to Ramah, and came to a great well that is in Sechu: and he asked and said, Where are Samuel and David? And one said, Behold, they be at Naioth in Ramah. And he went thither to Naioth in Ramah: and the Spirit of God was upon him also, and he went on, and prophesied, until he came to Naioth in Ramah. And he stripped off his clothes also, and prophesied before Samuel in like manner, and lay down naked all that day and all that night. Wherefore they say, Is Saul also among the prophets?" (1 Sam. 19:18–24).

2. "And David fled from Naioth in Ramah, and came and said before Jonathan, What have I done? what is mine iniquity? and what is my sin before thy father, that he seeketh my life? And he said unto him, God forbid; thou shalt not die: behold, my father will do nothing either great or small, but that he will shew it me: and why should my father hide this thing from me? it is not so. And David sware moreover, and said, Thy father certainly knoweth that I have found grace in thine eyes; and he saith, Let not Jonathan know this, lest he be grieved: but truly as the LORD liveth, and as thy soul liveth, there is but a step between me and death. Then said Jonathan unto David, Whatsoever thy soul desireth, I will even do it for thee" (2 Sam. 20:1–4).

3. "Then came David to Nob to Ahimelech the priest: and Ahimelech was afraid at the meeting of David, and said unto him, Why art thou alone, and no man with thee? And David said unto Ahimelech the priest, The king hath commanded me a business, and hath said unto me, Let no man know any thing of the business whereabout I send thee, and what I have commanded thee: and I have appointed my servants to such and such a place. Now therefore what is under thine hand? give me five loaves of bread in mine hand, or what there is present. And the priest answered David, and said, There is no common bread under mine hand, but there is hallowed bread;

if the young men have kept themselves at least from women. And David answered the priest, and said unto him, Of a truth women have been kept from us about these three days, since I came out, and the vessels of the young men are holy, and the bread is in a manner common, yea, though it were sanctified this day in the vessel. So the priest gave him hallowed bread: for there was no bread there but the shewbread, that was taken from before the LORD, to put hot bread in the day when it was taken away. Now a certain man of the servants of Saul was there that day, detained before the LORD; and his name was Doeg, an Edomite, the chiefest of the herdmen that belonged to Saul. And David said unto Ahimelech, And is there not here under thine hand spear or sword? for I have neither brought my sword nor my weapons with me, because the king's business required haste. And the priest said, The sword of Goliath the Philistine, whom thou slewest in the valley of Elah, behold, it is here wrapped in a cloth behind the ephod: if thou wilt take that, take it: for there is no other save that here. And David said, There is none like that; give it me" (2 Sam. 21:1–9).

4. "Remove from me the way of lying: and grant me thy law graciously" (Ps. 119:29).

5. "David therefore departed thence, and escaped to the cave Adullam: and when his brethren and all his father's house heard it, they went down thither to him. And every one that was in distress, and every one that was in debt, and every one that was discontented, gathered themselves unto him; and he became a captain over them: and there were with him about four hundred men" (1 Sam. 22:1–2).

6. "And David went thence to Mizpeh of Moab: and he said unto the king of Moab, Let my father and my mother, I pray thee, come forth, and be with you, till I know what God will do for me. And he brought them before the king of Moab: and they dwelt with him all the while that David was in the hold. And the prophet Gad said unto David, Abide not in the hold; depart, and get thee into the land of Judah. Then David departed, and came into the forest of Hareth" (1 Sam. 22:3–5).

7. "Then they told David, saying, Behold, the Philistines fight against Keilah, and they rob the threshingfloors. Therefore David enquired of the LORD, saying, Shall I go and smite these Philistines? And the LORD said unto David, Go, and smite the Philistines, and save Keilah. And David's men said unto him, Behold, we be afraid here in Judah: how much more then if we come to Keilah against the armies of the Philistines? Then David enquired of the LORD yet

again. And the LORD answered him and said, Arise, go down to Keilah; for I will deliver the Philistines into thine hand. So David and his men went to Keilah, and fought with the Philistines, and brought away their cattle, and smote them with a great slaughter. So David saved the inhabitants of Keilah. And it came to pass, when Abiathar the son of Ahimelech fled to David to Keilah, that he came down with an ephod in his hand. And it was told Saul that David was come to Keilah. And Saul said, God hath delivered him into mine hand; for he is shut in, by entering into a town that hath gates and bars. And Saul called all the people together to war, to go down to Keilah, to besiege David and his men. And David knew that Saul secretly practised mischief against him; and he said to Abiathar the priest, Bring hither the ephod. Then said David, O LORD God of Israel, thy servant hath certainly heard that Saul seeketh to come to Keilah, to destroy the city for my sake. Will the men of Keilah deliver me up into his hand? will Saul come down, as thy servant hath heard? O LORD God of Israel, I beseech thee, tell thy servant. And the LORD said, He will come down. Then said David, Will the men of Keilah deliver me and my men into the hand of Saul? And the LORD said, They will deliver thee up. Then David and his men, which were about six hundred, arose and departed out of Keilah, and went whithersoever they could go. And it was told Saul that David was escaped from Keilah; and he forbare to go forth" (1 Sam. 23:1–13).

8. "Not rendering evil for evil, or railing for railing: but contrari-wise blessing; knowing that ye are thereunto called, that ye should inherit a blessing" (1 Pet. 3:9).

9. "And David abode in the wilderness in strong holds, and remained in a mountain in the wilderness of Ziph. And Saul sought him every day, but God delivered him not into his hand. And David saw that Saul was come out to seek his life: and David was in the wilderness of Ziph in a wood. And Jonathan Saul's son arose, and went to David into the wood, and strengthened his hand in God. And he said unto him, Fear not: for the hand of Saul my father shall not find thee; and thou shalt be king over Israel, and I shall be next unto thee; and that also Saul my father knoweth. And they two made a covenant before the LORD: and David abode in the wood, and Jonathan went to his house" (1 Sam. 23:14–18).

10. "They were stoned, they were sawn asunder, were tempted, were slain with the sword: they wandered about in sheepskins and goatskins; being destitute, afflicted, tormented; (Of whom the world

was not worthy:) they wandered in deserts, and in mountains, and in dens and caves of the earth. And these all, having obtained a good report through faith, received not the promise: God having provided some better thing for us, that they without us should not be made perfect" (Heb. 11:37–40).

11. "And they arose, and went to Ziph before Saul: but David and his men were in the wilderness of Maon, in the plain on the south of Jeshimon. Saul also and his men went to seek him. And they told David; wherefore he came down into a rock, and abode in the wilderness of Maon. And when Saul heard that, he pursued after David in the wilderness of Maon. And Saul went on this side of the mountain, and David and his men on that side of the mountain: and David made haste to get away for fear of Saul; for Saul and his men compassed David and his men round about to take them. But there came a messenger unto Saul, saying, Haste thee, and come; for the Philistines have invaded the land. Wherefore Saul returned from pursuing after David, and went against the Philistines: therefore they called that place Selahammahlekoth. And David went up from thence, and dwelt in strong holds at Engedi" (1 Sam. 23:24–29).

12. "And they arose, and went to Ziph before Saul: but David and his men were in the wilderness of Maon, in the plain on the south of Jeshimon. Saul also and his men went to seek him. And they told David; wherefore he came down into a rock, and abode in the wilderness of Maon. And when Saul heard that, he pursued after David in the wilderness of Maon. And Saul went on this side of the mountain, and David and his men on that side of the mountain: and David made haste to get away for fear of Saul; for Saul and his men compassed David and his men round about to take them. But there came a messenger unto Saul, saying, Haste thee, and come; for the Philistines have invaded the land. Wherefore Saul returned from pursuing after David, and went against the Philistines: therefore they called that place Selahammahlekoth. And David went up from thence, and dwelt in strong holds at Engedi" (1 Sam. 24:4–7).

13. "And Samuel died; and all the Israelites were gathered together, and lamented him, and buried him in his house at Ramah. And David arose, and went down to the wilderness of Paran" (1 Sam. 25:1).

14. "I must work the works of him that sent me, while it is day: the night cometh, when no man can work" (John 9:4).

15. "And when Abigail saw David, she hasted, and lighted off the ass, and fell before David on her face, and bowed herself to the ground, And fell at his feet, and said, Upon me, my lord, upon me

let this iniquity be: and let thine handmaid, I pray thee, speak in thine audience, and hear the words of thine handmaid. Let not my lord, I pray thee, regard this man of Belial, even Nabal: for as his name is, so is he; Nabal is his name, and folly is with him: but I thine handmaid saw not the young men of my lord, whom thou didst send. Now therefore, my lord, as the LORD liveth, and as thy soul liveth, seeing the LORD hath withholden thee from coming to shed blood, and from avenging thyself with thine own hand, now let thine enemies, and they that seek evil to my lord, be as Nabal. And now this blessing which thine handmaid hath brought unto my lord, let it even be given unto the young men that follow my lord. I pray thee, forgive the trespass of thine handmaid: for the LORD will certainly make my lord a sure house; because my lord fighteth the battles of the LORD, and evil hath not been found in thee all thy days. Yet a man is risen to pursue thee, and to seek thy soul: but the soul of my lord shall be bound in the bundle of life with the LORD thy God; and the souls of thine enemies, them shall he sling out, as out of the middle of a sling. And it shall come to pass, when the LORD shall have done to my lord according to all the good that he hath spoken concerning thee, and shall have appointed thee ruler over Israel; That this shall be no grief unto thee, nor offence of heart unto my lord, either that thou hast shed blood causeless, or that my lord hath avenged himself: but when the LORD shall have dealt well with my lord, then remember thine handmaid" (1 Sam. 25:23–31).

16. "Then said Abishai to David, God hath delivered thine enemy into thine hand this day: now therefore let me smite him, I pray thee, with the spear even to the earth at once, and I will not smite him the second time. And David said to Abishai, Destroy him not: for who can stretch forth his hand against the LORD's anointed, and be guiltless? David said furthermore, As the LORD liveth, the LORD shall smite him; or his day shall come to die; or he shall descend into battle, and perish. The LORD forbid that I should stretch forth mine hand against the LORD's anointed: but, I pray thee, take thou now the spear that is at his bolster, and the cruse of water, and let us go. So David took the spear and the cruse of water from Saul's bolster; and they gat them away, and no man saw it, nor knew it, neither awaked: for they were all asleep; because a deep sleep from the LORD was fallen upon them" (1 Sam. 26:8–12).

17. "I the Lord search the heart, I try the reins, even to give every man according to his ways, and according to the fruit of his doings" (Jer. 17:10).

18. "And it came to pass, when David and his men were come to Ziklag on the third day, that the Amalekites had invaded the south, and Ziklag, and smitten Ziklag, and burned it with fire; And had taken the women captives, that were therein: they slew not any, either great or small, but carried them away, and went on their way. So David and his men came to the city, and, behold, it was burned with fire; and their wives, and their sons, and their daughters, were taken captives. Then David and the people that were with him lifted up their voice and wept, until they had no more power to weep. And David's two wives were taken captives, Ahinoam the Jezreelitess, and Abigail the wife of Nabal the Carmelite. And David was greatly distressed; for the people spake of stoning him, because the soul of all the people was grieved, every man for his sons and for his daughters: but David encouraged himself in the Lord his God. And David said to Abiathar the priest, Ahimelech's son, I pray thee, bring me hither the ephod. And Abiathar brought thither the ephod to David. And David enquired at the Lord, saying, Shall I pursue after this troop? shall I overtake them? And he answered him, Pursue: for thou shalt surely overtake them, and without fail recover all" (1 Sam. 30:1–8).

19. "For every one that useth milk is unskilful in the word of righteousness: for he is a babe. But strong meat belongeth to them that are of full age, even those who by reason of use have their senses exercised to discern both good and evil" (Heb. 5:13–14).

Chapter 5

1. "And they came to a place which was named Gethsemane: and he saith to his disciples, Sit ye here, while I shall pray. And he taketh with him Peter and James and John, and began to be sore amazed, and to be very heavy; And saith unto them, My soul is exceeding sorrowful unto death: tarry ye here, and watch. And he went forward a little, and fell on the ground, and prayed that, if it were possible, the hour might pass from him. And he said, Abba, Father, all things are possible unto thee; take away this cup from me: nevertheless not what I will, but what thou wilt. And he cometh, and findeth them sleeping, and saith unto Peter, Simon, sleepest thou? couldest not thou watch one hour? Watch ye and pray, lest ye enter into temptation. The spirit truly is ready, but the flesh is weak. And again he went away, and prayed, and spake the same words. And when he returned, he found them asleep again, (for their eyes were heavy,) neither wist they what to answer him. And he cometh the third time, and saith unto them, Sleep on now, and take your rest: it

is enough, the hour is come; behold, the Son of man is betrayed into the hands of sinners" (Mark 14:32–41).

2. "Who in the days of his flesh, when he had offered up prayers and supplications with strong crying and tears unto him that was able to save him from death, and was heard in that he feared; Though he were a Son, yet learned he obedience by the things which he suffered; And being made perfect, he became the author of eternal salvation unto all them that obey him" (Heb. 5:7–9).

3. "And thou shalt make it a perfume, a confection after the art of the apothecary, tempered together, pure and holy: And thou shalt beat some of it very small, and put of it before the testimony in the tabernacle of the congregation, where I will meet with thee: it shall be unto you most holy" (Exod. 30:35–36).

4. George Stormont, *Smith Wigglesworth: A Man Who Walked With God* (Tulsa, OK: Harrison House, 1989), 1, available at Google-Books, http://books.google.com/books?id=rDSKBloPwV8C&pg=PA1&lpg=PA1&dq=Wigglesworth,+I+am+going+to+burn+you+all+up,+until+there+is+no+more+Wigglesworth,+only+Jesus&source=bl&ots=uGPxN2oJa-&sig=BEDHfo1decQm_9nwTjFFfl2nqyo&hl=en&ei=JXKrTYDxO6LA0QHkt9D5CA&sa=X&oi=book_result&ct=result&resnum=1&ved=0CBQQ6AEwAA#v=onepage&q=Wigglesworth%2C%20I%20am%20going%20to%20burn%20you%20all%20up%2C%20until%20there%20is%20no%20more%20Wigglesworth%2C%20only%20Jesus&f=false, accessed April 17, 2011.

5. "I gave my back to the smiters, and my cheeks to them that plucked off the hair: I hid not my face from shame and spitting" (Isa. 50:6).

6. "Create in me a clean heart, O God; and renew a right spirit within me. Cast me not away from thy presence; and take not thy holy spirit from me. Restore unto me the joy of thy salvation; and uphold me with thy free spirit. Then will I teach transgressors thy ways; and sinners shall be converted unto thee. Deliver me from bloodguiltiness, O God, thou God of my salvation: and my tongue shall sing aloud of thy righteousness. O Lord, open thou my lips; and my mouth shall shew forth thy praise. For thou desirest not sacrifice; else would I give it: thou delightest not in burnt offering. The sacrifices of God are a broken spirit: a broken and a contrite heart, O God, thou wilt not despise" (Ps. 51:10–17)7. Stormont, *Smith Wigglesworth: A Man Who Walked with God*, 44.

8. "As the hart panteth after the water brooks, so panteth my soul after thee, O God. My soul thirsteth for God, for the living God:

when shall I come and appear before God? y tears have been my meat day and night, while they continually say unto me, Where is thy God? When I remember these things, I pour out my soul in me: for I had gone with the multitude, I went with them to the house of God, with the voice of joy and praise, with a multitude that kept holyday. Why art thou cast down, O my soul? and why art thou disquieted in me? hope thou in God: for I shall yet praise him for the help of his countenance. O my God, my soul is cast down within me: therefore will I remember thee from the land of Jordan, and of the Hermonites, from the hill Mizar. Deep calleth unto deep at the noise of thy waterspouts: all thy waves and thy billows are gone over me. Yet the Lord will command his lovingkindness in the day time, and in the night his song shall be with me, and my prayer unto the God of my life. I will say unto God my rock, Why hast thou forgotten me? why go I mourning because of the oppression of the enemy? As with a sword in my bones, mine enemies reproach me; while they say daily unto me, Where is thy God? Why art thou cast down, O my soul? and why art thou disquieted within me? hope thou in God: for I shall yet praise him, who is the health of my countenance, and my God" (Ps. 42:1–11).

9. Lester Sumrall, *Pioneers of Faith* (South Bend, IN: Sumrall Publishing, 1995), 162–164.

Chapter 6

1. "And it came to pass, as she continued praying before the Lord, that Eli marked her mouth. Now Hannah, she spake in her heart; only her lips moved, but her voice was not heard: therefore Eli thought she had been drunken. And Eli said unto her, How long wilt thou be drunken? put away thy wine from thee. And Hannah answered and said, No, my lord, I am a woman of a sorrowful spirit: I have drunk neither wine nor strong drink, but have poured out my soul before the Lord. Count not thine handmaid for a daughter of Belial: for out of the abundance of my complaint and grief have I spoken hitherto. Then Eli answered and said, Go in peace: and the God of Israel grant thee thy petition that thou hast asked of him" (1 Sam. 1:12–17).

2. "And Jesus returned in the power of the Spirit into Galilee: and there went out a fame of him through all the region round about. And he taught in their synagogues, being glorified of all. And he came to Nazareth, where he had been brought up: and, as his custom was, he went into the synagogue on the sabbath day, and

stood up for to read. And there was delivered unto him the book of the prophet Esaias. And when he had opened the book, he found the place where it was written, The Spirit of the Lord is upon me, because he hath anointed me to preach the gospel to the poor; he hath sent me to heal the brokenhearted, to preach deliverance to the captives, and recovering of sight to the blind, to set at liberty them that are bruised, To preach the acceptable year of the Lord. And he closed the book, and he gave it again to the minister, and sat down. And the eyes of all them that were in the synagogue were fastened on him. And he began to say unto them, This day is this scripture fulfilled in your ears. And all bare him witness, and wondered at the gracious words which proceeded out of his mouth. And they said, Is not this Joseph's son? And he said unto them, Ye will surely say unto me this proverb, Physician, heal thyself: whatsoever we have heard done in Capernaum, do also here in thy country. And he said, Verily I say unto you, No prophet is accepted in his own country. But I tell you of a truth, many widows were in Israel in the days of Elias, when the heaven was shut up three years and six months, when great famine was throughout all the land; But unto none of them was Elias sent, save unto Sarepta, a city of Sidon, unto a woman that was a widow. And many lepers were in Israel in the time of Eliseus the prophet; and none of them was cleansed, saving Naaman the Syrian. And all they in the synagogue, when they heard these things, were filled with wrath, And rose up, and thrust him out of the city, and led him unto the brow of the hill whereon their city was built, that they might cast him down headlong. But he passing through the midst of them went his way" (Luke 4:14–30).

3. "Let us go forth therefore unto him without the camp, bearing his reproach" (Heb. 13:13).

4. "And when Jesus was entered into Capernaum, there came unto him a centurion, beseeching him, And saying, Lord, my servant lieth at home sick of the palsy, grievously tormented. And Jesus saith unto him, I will come and heal him. The centurion answered and said, Lord, I am not worthy that thou shouldest come under my roof: but speak the word only, and my servant shall be healed. For I am a man under authority, having soldiers under me: and I say to this man, Go, and he goeth; and to another, Come, and he cometh; and to my servant, Do this, and he doeth it. When Jesus heard it, he marvelled, and said to them that followed, Verily I say unto you, I have not found so great faith, no, not in Israel" (Matt. 8:5–10).

5. "And, behold, a woman of Canaan came out of the same coasts, and cried unto him, saying, Have mercy on me, O Lord, thou son of David; my daughter is grievously vexed with a devil. But he answered her not a word. And his disciples came and besought him, saying, Send her away; for she crieth after us. But he answered and said, I am not sent but unto the lost sheep of the house of Israel. Then came she and worshipped him, saying, Lord, help me. But he answered and said, It is not meet to take the children's bread, and to cast it to dogs. And she said, Truth, Lord: yet the dogs eat of the crumbs which fall from their masters' table. Then Jesus answered and said unto her, O woman, great is thy faith: be it unto thee even as thou wilt. And her daughter was made whole from that very hour" (Matt. 15:22–28).

OTHER BOOKS BY THE AUTHOR

Answering the Call to the Ministry (Available in Danish)

Insecurity in Ministry

Communion and the New Covenant

Fear Not

Everyday Promises of Jesus

Anointing for Endurance

Flies in the Ointment

Discerning Ditches in the Last Days

Seven Benefits of Righteousness

Vessel unto Honor

Sex, Fantasy and Reality

Absent Without Leave

Mentoring in Life and Ministry

Understanding Seasons in Life and Ministry

Faith Under Fire

ABOUT THE AUTHOR

REVEREND TUNDE BOLANTA is the General Overseer of Restoration Ministries. He has an apostolic call to the nations with a prophetic cutting edge. The meetings witness salvation, healing and prophetic manifestation.

He is the founder of Mercy Home Orphanage, Women and Youth Empowerment Centre, Mercy Home Clinic and Maternity Centre for community health care and free deliveries for teenage mothers. Other outreaches of the Ministry include Schools, Media and International Outreach.

He is married to Christian Eleojo Bolanta and they are blessed with three children: Nathan, Sharon, and Ephraim. They live in Kaduna, Nigeria, where they oversee many churches.

CONTACT THE AUTHOR

TUNDE BOLANTA
P.O. BOX 1485
800001
KADUNA, NIGERIA
WWW.RBCMONLINE.ORG

PERSONAL NOTES